Standing Up To Supernanny

Jennie Bristow

with

The Institute of Ideas Parents' Forum

SOCIETAS
essays in political
& cultural criticism

imprint-academic.com

Published in the UK by Societas
Imprint Academic, PO Box 200, Exeter EX5 5YX, UK

Published in the USA by Societas
Imprint Academic, Philosophy Documentation Center
PO Box 7147, Charlottesville, VA 22906-7147, USA

ISBN 9781845401702

A CIP catalogue record for this book is available from the
British Library and US Library of Congress

Contents

Acknowledgements

This book would not have been possible without the intellectual and moral support of many people. Many thanks to Jane Sandeman and the members of the Parents' Forum; to Claire Fox and the Institute of Ideas team; and to *spiked*. For their interest and editorial input, thanks to Veronique Baxter, Frank Furedi, Ellie Lee, and the team at Societas. Above all thanks to my family for constantly bringing home why this matters.

Jennie Bristow, Kent 2009

Notes on Contributors

Jennie Bristow writes the monthly *Guide to Subversive Parenting* for the online publication *spiked*, and is a frequent guest on Radio Four's *Woman's Hour*. She is co-author, with Frank Furedi, of *Licensed to Hug: How child protection policies are poisoning the relationship between the generations and damaging the voluntary sector* (Civitas 2008), and author of *Maybe I Do: marriage and commitment in singleton society* (Academy of Ideas 2002). Bristow edits the website Parents With Attitude <http://www.parentswithattitude.com> and the BPAS journal *Abortion Review* <http://www.abortionreview.org>. She is currently researching the changing contours of inter-generational relations.

Dr Val Gillies is a reader at London South Bank University, and author of *Marginalised Mothers: Exploring Working Class Experiences of Parenting*. London and New York: Routledge (2006).

Dr Helene Guldberg is co-founder and director of *spiked* <http://www.spiked-online.com> and author of *Reclaiming Childhood: Freedom and play in an age of fear*. London and New York: Routledge (2009).

Christina Hardyment is a writer and historian with special interest in family and domestic matters, and author of *Dream Babies: Childcare advice from John Locke to Gina Ford*. London: Francis Lincoln Publishers (2007).

Jennifer Howze is lifestyle editor at *Times Online*, and edits *The Times*'s parenting blog Alpha Mummy www.alphamummy.com

Tracey Jensen is a doctoral student at the Open University.

Dr Ellie Lee is a lecturer in social policy at the University of Kent; co-ordinator of Parenting Culture Studies <http://www.parenting

culturestudies.org>; and author of *Abortion, Motherhood and Mental Health: Medicalising reproduction in the United States and Great Britain.* New York: Aldine de Gruyter (2003).

Dr Jan Macvarish is a researcher at the University of Kent, with an interest in the sociology of family life and intimate relationships.

Nancy McDermott is a journalist based in Brooklyn, New York, and chair of the Advisory Board of Park Slope Parents, the second largest parenting group in the USA.

Jane Sandeman is the founder and convenor of the Institute of Ideas Parents' Forum <http://www.instituteofideas.com/events/parentsforum.html>.

Zoe Williams is a columnist for the *Guardian*, with a particular interest in feminism and babies.

Foreword

As I write, yet another 'landmark' report has been published claiming that British children are in a worse state than any in Europe, and that parents are to blame. *A Good Childhood: Searching for values in a competitive age*, commissioned by the Church of England Children's Society (Layard and Dunn 2009; The Children's Society 2009a), contains the standard list of solutions to this apparent problem of degenerate kids and half-assed parenting — parenting education, parenting programmes and psychological support.

The report, as with many others of its ilk, claims to be reflecting the views of children — whether it does this is debatable. But one voice that is rarely even solicited in the contemporary debate about parenting is that of parents. It is accepted that parents are the villains, incompetents and saviours of our ailing society, who are waiting stage left to receive the next policy initiative thrown in their direction.

This situation is the backdrop to the Institute of Ideas Parents' Forum. Three years ago I, along with two other mothers who also had children at pre-school and primary school, decided that we wanted to do something more than moan about how many of these initiatives impacted on our lives and made us feel that we were always doing something wrong. We wanted to understand why they were happening, why we weren't allowed to just bring up our children how we wanted to, and whether there were any other people — parents and non-parents — who felt the same way. And we found that yes, there were people out there who did want to question the idea that there was some exact science to being a parent that only the experts could understand and prescribe. People did want to understand why intervening in something as intimate as family relationships had become one of the main planks of social policy

From the small monthly discussions of the Parents' Forum, we developed a debate strand for the annual Battle of Ideas festival in November 2008, under the headline 'The Battle for the Family'. This successful series of debates, kindly sponsored by the Economic and Social Research Council (ESRC), brought together academics, journalists, policy-makers and parents to discuss why parenting has become such a key issue today, and what the impact of this shift has been on the broader politics of the family. Many of the panellists involved in 'The Battle for the Family' have contributed their reflections on the parenting debate to this book, and we thank them for their ongoing work and support in this area.

Jennie Bristow, the main author of *Standing up to Supernanny*, is a key member of the Parents' Forum, and this book brings together many of the discussions we have been pursuing for the past three years. For us, the key point is that, despite the continual bad publicity, the family remains, for most people, 'a haven in a heartless world'. People still want to have children, and when they do they realise how brilliant it is. Yes it is hard work, yes it does turn your life upside down—but most parents wouldn't change it for anything. And this is what we are working to defend.

In an age of parent-bashing policy and intrusive expert advice, Jennie argues that we must reclaim the 'muddled messiness' that is family life. This means that there is not an exact science to being a parent to your children: there is not some recipe out there that tells you the exact amount of love you should give to your children, the exact way you should discipline your children, the exact authority you should exercise as a parent. You make the rules—for your children your parenting style is the right style. The book is a clarion call for parents not to get persuaded by the experts that there is a recipe to be assiduously followed which will produce the perfect child. As Jennie concludes, we are adults, not children to be bossed around. We should and must take responsibility for our own families and stand in solidarity with other parents.

I hope that this book is the start of a movement where parents find their voice and their confidence and reclaim the terrain that is rightfully theirs.

Jane Sandeman, March 2009

PART ONE

Standing up to Supernanny

Chapter One

Introduction

It should be a wonderful time to be a parent. Standards of living are higher than ever before; women no longer have to choose between work and motherhood; thanks to modern contraception we can plan the number and timing of our children, ensuring that we only have kids if we want and when we want. Men bathe babies, change nappies, attend the birth of their children and can only expect a meal on the table if they cook it themselves — and they are encouraged to feel good about themselves for doing all this.

So why is it that with all of these choices, all the flexibility, equality, love and respect we have come to expect as our right, parenthood comes as such a shock to the system? How can the arrival of one small extra person into our lives send the world topsy-turvy, transforming the savvy, confident people we were into a craven mass of earnest anxiety, hooked on the desire to do the right thing while our legs chafe in the shackles of Being Home? Has nothing really changed after all; has sexual inequality been suspended only for childless people, just waiting to come around again once we embark on parenthood? Or are we just hopelessly inept, and insufferably selfish, individuals?

John Bowlby, the famous child psychiatrist who in the middle of the last century popularised the notion that babies separated from their mothers would suffer tremendous trauma, has preached about the tremendous hard work involved in looking after small children, including giving them enough time and attention which 'means sacrificing other interests and other activities'. 'For many people today these are unpalatable truths', he said in 1980 (Bowlby 1988, p2). The idea that modern parents simply aren't up to the job, that they can't handle the selflessness of looking after children or the responsibility of bringing them up without great swathes of official advice and support, has become a key feature of government policy and official advice that trickles down through the Department of Health, the Department for Children, Schools and Families, the Home Office, and any other Department that might have anything to say about parents and children.

Parenthood, we are continually told, requires a massive adjustment to our lives, emotions, and relationships, and we have to be taught how to deal with that. 'There's something very special and exciting about being alone for the first time with your new baby, but it can also be frightening', states the first page of *Birth to Five*, the Department of Health's guide to 'everything you need to know about becoming a parent':

> This is when you begin to realise that you can never go back. You're now responsible for a new human being. The responsibility may seem much too big. … Think of these first few pages as a guide to the basic information you'll need to survive (DH 2007, p3).

The government-funded helpline *Parentline Plus* has as its tagline 'because instructions aren't included' (Parentline Plus 2009). In November 2007, the launch of the government's £30million national parenting academy made official the idea that parenthood is really something that people should be trained in by qualified practitioners according to a particular method of 'parenting', before parents themselves are let loose upon their own children (NAPP 2007).

Anyone who has had children will know that it's not all a bed of roses; that there are tough times, tantrums, ear infections, arguments, and moments when you just don't know what you are doing. But can it really be so bad that we need counselling to get us through it? Are we really so bad that we need to be trained? In a word: No. It is a myth that today's parents are hopeless, and even more of a myth that they don't try hard. In many ways, the problem is that we try *too hard* at being parents—we're too diligent, too conscientious, too hopeful of great outcomes and clear rewards, to the point where we lose ourselves in trying to provide some kind of professional service to our children. This doesn't help children, and for parents it's a disaster zone. We make our lives miserably tough, for no reason other than that we think this is what we should be doing. This book is about finding a new way to look at family life today, which starts not from political slogans and unattainable ideals about what it should be, but understands and defends what it is, in all its muddled messiness.

What's new?

A lot has changed about the family: marriage and divorce rates, family size, geographical mobility and, in particular, women's role in society and their expectations of their lives. We need to make sense of these changes and what they mean for us. But the fundamental relationships of family life, the emotional intimacy between parents, and between parents and children, have not changed all that much—and these relationships need to be defended against the bad faith and meddling of policymakers and parenting 'experts'.

Many commentators have noted how, in recent decades, parents and parenting have been thrust into the public, political spotlight—and that this has not been good news for parents. 'Until very, very recently ... parents counted for nothing in the world of politics', notes Maureen Freely in *The Parent Trap* (Freely 2000, p1). 'Childhood has moved much more into the public eye in the last twenty years', writes Oxford historian Christina Hardyment in her classic account of baby-care advice over the past 200 years:

> The hungry maw of the 24-hour rolling news culture delights in broadcasting the bad news about parenting. ... Moral panics over children abound, the outward and visible signs of a widespread vacuum in adult values. ... Guilt is the hallmark of the age (Hardyment 2007, p283).

The sociologist Frank Furedi has argued that relentless official pressure upon parents to do everything right has resulted in a process of 'Paranoid Parenting', which has made adults increasingly insecure about how they relate to children in general and crippled with anxiety when it comes to raising their own. According to Furedi, the notion of 'parental causality'—the idea that every little thing a parent does has a defining impact upon their child's life—has become both a widely-held cultural belief and a central plank of parenting policy, with the effect that parenting becomes a fraught pursuit with impossible goals (Furedi 2001). In the USA, a critique of the culture of 'intensive mothering', begun by the academic Sharon Hays (1996) in *The Cultural Contradictions of Motherhood*, has spawned a scholarly fightback. Susan Douglas and Meredith Michaels, writing about 'The Mommy Myth', have attacked the 'chasm between the ridiculous, honey-hued ideals of perfect motherhood in the mass media and the reality of mothers' everyday lives' (Douglas and Michaels 2004, p2), and Judith Warner (2006) labels contemporary Anglo-American parenting culture 'Perfect Madness'.

The combination of a cultural obsession with 'perfect parenting' and a policy framework that sees parents both as the cause of all society's problems and a solution to its ills, has led to an immense amount of pressure upon parents to conform to a range of different, and often contradictory, standards. Our children's educational success apparently lies in the quality and amount of homework help we give them, yet at the same time we are supposed to create a relaxed and warm home environment in which the 'pushy parent' does more harm than good. Keeping children safe from all possible harm is deemed to be the most important thing; yet we are then criticised for raising a generation of 'cotton wool kids' by failing to let them play outside or walk to school, harming their development and making them fat.

Falling for it

Having taken the leap into parenthood, we are generally a mature and responsible group of people who worry rather more about our children's future and wellbeing than we do our own—making us particularly vulnerable to criticisms that we are not 'doing it right', and to the endless stream of advice about the numerous ways in which we could be doing better by our kids. Hands up those who spent their twenties laughing off official warnings about the dangers of drinking, smoking, drugs, eating junk food, living in a city—only to find, with the first rush of pregnancy, that all advice had to be taken totally seriously, even if you knew deep down that it was rubbish. There's something about having kids that makes you think you should grow up; and in today's uptight, unimaginative culture, growing up means conforming to the latest line in lifestyle correctness.

Our own experience tells us, only too clearly, that parenting has become politicised and that this has made our role, as parents, more difficult. But when a number of writers from diverse political perspectives and from both sides of the Atlantic reveal the scale of this shift, from child-rearing as something you just did to 'parenting' as a task that you have to do exactly right, this indicates that something should be done. For parents, for children, even for policymakers—it is in nobody's interests to have a generation of adults so worn down and confused by the rules and pressures of perfect parenting that they lose the ability to enjoy their own children and make decisions about how best to bring them up. So why aren't we standing up for ourselves a bit more?

Mommy rebels

Some mothers-turned-writers, or writers-turned-mothers, have reacted to the parenting pressure-cooker through advocating sheer rebellion. In *Confessions of a Bad Mother* (2005), Stephanie Calman sticks two fingers up to the orthodoxy of perfect parenting by recounting her own tales of hedonism and bad temper, including drinking during pregnancy, demanding a C-section, and swearing at the kids. The Bad Mothers Club, a website founded by Calman in 2003, 'seeks to provide a genuine alternative to the content of mainstream websites and women's magazines, much of which contributes to women's fear that they are somehow inadequate, as mothers and as people'. The website 'is designed to be a place where people can express their true feelings about parenting, families, relationships and Life in general' (Bad Mothers Club 2009). Or, as it turns out, go online and swear a lot about the latest thing about parenting that has really pissed you off.

Calman is generally pictured with a glass of wine at her lips and an expression of mischievous defiance on her face. And if the 'Fuck It' philosophy of the Bad Mothers Club hasn't yet permeated the ranks of middle-class mominess, the drinking bit has. When the Department of Health, in May 2007, changed its advice to pregnant women from recommending no more than two units of alcohol a week to recommending no alcohol at all (BBC News Online 2007: 25 May; Alcohol Policy UK 2007; Bristow 2007), mummy-commentators from across the UK press lined up to confess that they had enjoyed the occasional glass of wine in pregnancy. When, in August 2007, a privately-run chain of residential alcoholism treatment centres warned that the pressure of looking after children in the school holidays was leading to a peak in the number of admissions from mothers (*Daily Telegraph* 2007), a comment piece by Kishanda Fulford in the *Daily Telegraph* fumed: '[O]f course we are driven to drink … I would be lying if I said I didn't look forward to a glass of wine as I wind down at the end of the day. Motherhood is a perpetual war zone' (Fulford 2007). In the USA, there are tales of 'cocktail playgroups' started up by suburban moms, which serve juice to the kids and martinis to 'increasing numbers of bored, frustrated or just plain thirsty mothers [who] are flaunting their cocktail playgroups as a symbol of their liberation from domestic drudgery' (Allen-Mills 2006).

From the hugely successful US series *Desperate Housewives* to newspaper columns and novels charting the life of a 'Slummy Mummy' who can't keep the house tidy or balance the books and occasionally sneaks the odd cigarette (Neill 2007), parental rebellion has reached popular culture too. The more intense the pressure becomes to parent our children perfectly, the more this ideal is mocked as unrealistic and, frankly, undesirable. Parents, we are beginning to understand, have lives too; and like the teenager who is continually told not to drink, smoke, have sex or hang about on street corners, the more parents are presented with rules about how to live their daily lives, the more they have to rebel against. This is all pretty heartening stuff—particularly when you realise that your own cohort of 'mommy group' mums would probably be happier in the pub than in the living room, and that they sometimes feed their kids crisps and chicken nuggets too.

A grown-up debate

But. Apart from a small minority of very young mums and dads, parents are not teenagers, and they shouldn't have to rebel at all. The rise of the rebellious parent in many ways represents the most disturbing feature of today's obsessive parenting culture: the transformation of parents into childlike figures, forced to seek permission and approval from official sources for how we conduct our everyday lives. From the moment we get pregnant with our first child, we become infantilised ourselves—counselled about how difficult parenting is, bombarded with advice about everything from all quarters, continually monitored about how well we are coping with the nigh-on impossible 'job' that parenting has become. In treating parents like children, officials and experts assume that it is their role to raise our families, because how could mere mortals possibly be trusted to do it properly? So we are told, in both the nicest and the sternest possible ways, to move over and make space in our families for whoever-knows-best-today.

This book aims to re-pose the discussion about parenting today, situating parents as the authorities on their own family lives, and resisting the assumption that parents are not up to the job. It is about challenging the myths surrounding modern parenthood, and asking why policymakers refuse to face up to many of the realities of family life today. It is about the need for privacy, a space in which we and our children can be ourselves and be with each other, shielded from instruction by parenting manuals, reality TV shows, and the authorities. Above all, it is a call for solidarity: for parents to stick together in the face of the pressures that try to divide us into yummy-mummies versus slummy-mummies, breast-feeders versus bottle-feeders, organic healthy-eaters versus junk-food mums. Parents, like children, are all different. But we have more in common with each other than with the massed ranks of experts trying to tell us how to be.

Chapter Two

Parents as Villains

Look at the viewing figures for *Supernanny*. There's no shortage of people who want to be bossed around a bit. *Louise Casey, the UK government's 'Respect Tsar', talking to the Daily Telegraph* (Sylvester and Thomson 2007).

The first time I ever watched the hit UK TV series *Supernanny*, I spent the entire fifty-minute hour shouting at the TV. Who did this woman think she was, barging into complete strangers' lives, bossing them around, patronising them, talking about them behind their back to an audience of millions? And who were these people, who asked this woman into their homes, presented themselves for verbal castration, and embraced the humiliation of exposing the chaos of their private space to an audience of millions?

The second time I watched *Supernanny*, I cried. This was a particularly heart-rending episode, featuring a young couple whose four-year-old son was exhibiting violent, uncontrolled tantrums, related to, it transpired, the loss of his brother to cot death two years previously. But what upset me the most was that this time, I felt that I understood its appeal. Who invited Supernanny home? We did. Why? Because we feel so inadequate as parents, so open to the suggestion that we are somehow failing our kids, that we willingly usher self-styled parenting experts into our lives, even when it means giving up autonomy, privacy, and basic self-respect.

The Channel Four series *Supernanny* has achieved that dubious moniker of 'Hit reality TV show'. Supernanny herself, Jo Frost, is everywhere—in the United States, where the show has become prime time viewing, publishing books on childcare, running private consultations with desperate parents through her 'B4UGo-Ga-Ga' service (Jo Frost 2009), looming out the back of a box of Kelloggs Cornflakes to endorse the idea that breakfast is, indeed, the most important meal of the day. The show's success is not surprising: anything calling itself reality TV currently seems to be guaranteed a mass audience, while in the publishing world, 'expert' childcare advice has become an industry in its own right. But to dismiss *Supernanny* as just, say, *Wife Swap* for parents, or Gina Ford on telly, would be too glib. Like Heineken in those old adverts, *Supernanny* reaches the parts that other bits of child-rearing advice can't reach.

Writing in the *Sunday Telegraph* (London) in April 2007, Jenny McCartney criticised children's minister Beverley Hughes for using the popularity of TV programmes such as *Supernanny* and its Big Brother-style competitor *House of Tiny Tearaways* as evidence of popular support for the government's new national parenting academy, launched in November 2007:

> [T]he real reason that most of us enjoy watching such shows is so that we can feel pleasurably superior to the participants in the flamboyant domestic mess on screen, not because we want Government supernannies rapping at our own doors (McCartney 2007).

True enough, to the extent that most parents would rather share their personal space with a cool-headed-but-cuddly Jo Frost than with any kind of health visitor/social worker/other official wolf-in-sheep's-clothing. It also helps that for most of us, Jo Frost exists only on TV rather than on our doorstep. But while the trials undergone by many of the families in *Supernanny*'s Sandpit of Shame do make you look rather more fondly at your own (relatively angelic) children, the show's appeal has a sharper dimension than mere voyeurism — as Tracey Jensen explains, in her reflection on the parenting debate in Part Two of this book. It's not like *How Clean Is Your House?*, where people's willingness to air their dirty laundry (and everything else) in public shows that housekeeping standards don't really matter as a mark of who you are. People invite *Supernanny* home because, conversely, the behaviour of your kids and the quality of your parenting skills is seen to be so important that it trumps every other traditional family value: pride, confidence, privacy. There is a sense that what *Supernanny* does is of real, lasting value; and if *Beyond the Naughty Step*, the 'real-life' follow-on about life when Supernanny leaves, shows parents reverting to some of their inept old ways, it is assumed that they will retain some lasting benefit from their Time With Jo Jo.

The question of whether *Supernanny*'s effect on family harmony is any more real or lasting than, say, the plaster put on houses in those miracle-DIY shows that falls of the walls the minute the cameras leave, is rarely asked. But we should note that it cannot be assumed that *Supernanny* does anything it says on the tin. We think that the programme shows us how the children involved actually behave — it could simply be showing us how they behave when provoked into various artificial and unreasonable situations at the time of filming. In 2006, a Scottish family reportedly sought legal advice after appearing on the programme, claiming that it had been edited to make their family look worse than they were, and that members of their community had shunned them as a result (UPI News Service 2006). Anecdotal evidence, media experience and common sense is enough to tell you that reality TV does not portray 'reality', but 50 minutes or so of carefully-edited highlights. *Supernanny* doesn't necessarily offer practical, useful advice to couples about how to cope with the aspect of their children's behaviour that they are most worried about on an everyday level — the programme could just as easily be offering a pre-packaged advice plan and filming the bits of participants' family life that seem to be in need of that particular advice.

But hey, this is telly — and the bottom line is that the real impact on people matters far less than the symbolic effect upon the audience. Whatever happens 'beyond the naughty step', the symbolic success of *Supernanny* is in cementing the idea that parents really want and need a 'third person' in their relationship to help with the allegedly hellish torment of raising their children. The background to this idea is that parents are doing a terrible job, and that the consequences of leaving them to raise their children in the time-honoured fashion would be disastrous for society.

Parents: A bad news story?

'Another week, another child gunned down on the streets of Britain'. So began a gloomy column by Julia Hartley-Brewer in the *Sunday Express*, following the tragic shooting of 11-year-old Rhys Jones, who became an accidental target in a battle between teenage gangs (Hartley-Brewer 2007). For Hartley-Brewer, this tragedy was an instant metaphor for the fatal consequences of a generation of lawless children brought up by feckless parents, too incapable and unwilling to lay down basic rules of discipline. 'We all know who they are', she continued:

> We see them when we're out and about. And if we're lucky we don't have to live next door to them or on the same sink estate. But you only have to watch five minutes of a TV series such as *Supernanny* or *Brat Camp* to know why they behave as they do. This isn't about zero tolerance policing so much as zero tolerance parenting.

It may seem unfair to pick on Julia Hartley-Brewer when every-body, from prime minister Gordon Brown to the chatterati in every other corner of the UK media, pounced upon this young boy's mur-der to make their particular moral point about how we stop society going to Hell in a handcart. But just as this *Sunday Express* journalist had no qualms about using a dead child as a basis to air her general prejudices about rubbish parents, so her arguments are fair game as representations of more widely-shared misconceptions.

Hartley-Brewer's opening line—'Another week, another child gunned down on the streets of Britain'—gains in melodramatic effect what it loses in actual fact. The implication is that we are living in a war zone, in which children are lucky if they make it home from school without a bullet in the head. In fact, the death of young people—indeed, any people—as a result of gun crime in Britain is remarkably low. As one BBC report explains (Casciani 2008: 31 Janu-ary), during 2007, nine young people lost their lives in shootings— tragedies all, but it is surely a mark of how unlike the New York Bronx Britain is that every one of these deaths can be mourned *ad nauseam* by the national press. In fact, the number of young people killed in violent crime at all 'is relatively small and volatile':

> In 1995, 44 people between five and 16 years old were victims of homicide. In 2005–06 the number was less than half of that—and during the in-between years it varied wildly (Casciani 2008: 31 January).

The notion that young people are increasingly dangerous and in danger from ever-more violent crimes is so preciously held that it is perhaps naïve to think that something so trivial as statistical evi-dence could stand in the way of a good story. But let's face facts here: Whatever the problems with Britain's youth, it is not that they are about to kill themselves and each other in a haze of gunfire.

Indeed, we seem to be rather good at keeping our kids alive today. A UNICEF report on 'child well-being in rich countries' produced in 2007 indicates just how well today's children fare compared to previous generations:

> By almost every available measure, the great majority of children born in today's developed societies enjoy unprecedented levels of health and safety. Almost within living memory, one child in every five in the cities of Europe could be expected to die before his or her fifth birthday; today that risk is less than one in a hun-dred. Loss of life among older children is even more uncommon; fewer than one in every 10,000 young people die before the age of 19 as a result of accident, murder, suicide or violence. This, too,

represents an historically unheard of level of safety (UNICEF 2007, p13).

At one end of the spectrum is a dramatic decline in infant mortality; at the other is the continued rise in life expectancy. In 2002, life expectancy at birth for females born in the UK was 81 years, compared with 76 years for males, and is projected to go on rising until 2020. By way of comparison: in 1901, life expectancy was 49 years for women and 45 years for men (ONS 2004). We protect our children from illness: in the UK, where childhood vaccination is voluntary, 87% of children aged 12–23 months have been vaccinated against the major vaccine-preventable diseases, despite the panic about the Measles, Mumps and Rubella (MMR) vaccine set in motion by the disgraced doctor Andrew Wakefield along with sections of the medical and mainstream press (UNICEF 2007, p15; Fitzpatrick 2004). And as UNICEF also notes, the United Kingdom, along with Sweden, the Netherlands and Italy, has reduced 'the incidence of deaths from accidents and injuries to the remarkably low level of fewer than 10 per 10,000' (UNICEF 2007, p15).

You could reasonably argue, of course, that parents cannot take sole credit for these massive improvements to children's health and safety: that broad patterns of social development, alongside specific social policies, play a decisive role in bringing down infant mortality rates and effective immunisations. But you can't have it both ways. If parents are to be (unfairly) blamed for a (non-existent) wave of violent teenage murder, they should at least be able to claim credit for the real, demonstrable change in children's wellbeing: that more of them stay alive and well for longer. I mean, this is a good news story, right? With statistics like these, how bad can parents (or children) actually be?

This is where the Bad Parenting discussion departs from reality into the fantasy world of reality TV, where the scope of the problem with today's kids and their parents is suddenly, drastically expanded. Take Hartley-Brewer's thesis 'you only have to watch five minutes of a TV series such as *Supernanny* or *Brat Camp* to know why [these murderous, gun-toting teenage gangsters] behave as they do'. In the blink of a cursor, a parent's struggle to control a toddler tantrum is the defining reason behind the (non-)wave of teenage gun murders. For UNICEF, meanwhile, the solid statistics showing the health of children in rich countries are themselves a problem, as they only mask other—less clearly definable—bad news. So its report bemoans the fact that, due to a lack of common systems of measurement between countries, it has been impossible to include 'some indicator of the level of child abuse and neglect in each nation':

> In total, approximately 3,500 children (under the age of 15) die every year in the OECD countries from maltreatment, physical abuse, and neglect. Traffic accidents, drownings, falls, fires and poisoning carry this total to more than 20,000 child deaths each year. These may not be large figures in relation to the total populations of young people in the OECD countries. But ... such figures need to be read in the light of the unimaginable anguish and grief of the families concerned, and of the fact that the number of deaths is but the tip of an iceberg of trauma and disability (UNICEF 2007, p16).

A small number of children do suffer from appalling abuse, at the hands of family members or other trusted adults. Others suffer from accidents or illness, which devastate their lives and those of their loved ones. But as UNICEF is grudgingly forced to admit, when looked at in perspective, as a proportion of total populations and in historical comparison, these are not large numbers. In fact, they are quite tiny. The great health and wellbeing enjoyed by the majority of children becomes the subject of miserablist speculation — 'the tip of an iceberg of trauma' — rather than a cause for congratulation. Meanwhile, the report's assertion that British children rank lowest out of 21 countries in terms of 'emotional well-being' (whatever that means) has subsequently been recycled through countless news articles and comment pieces, used to justify everything from Tory party policy developments to head teachers' calls for reform of the educational testing regime in schools (BBC 2007, 26 March and 5 May).

It is a sign of the times that the bad news side of the UNICEF report was accepted so readily, while the good news got barely a look-in. In the same way, cases of the most appalling child abuse, such as that of Victoria Climbie in 2000 or 'Baby P' in 2008, lead directly to media discussions and policy initiatives that assume child abuse to be endemic within all families. In November 2008, following the conviction of Baby P's mother, her boyfriend and another man for causing the death of this 17-month-old boy, who had over 50 separate injuries to his body, the media erupted with breast-beating commentary about how and why this could have happened, and what it says about families in our society. A month later, research claiming that 'one in ten' children suffer from abuse each year (Gilbert *et al* 2009) made the front page of the mainstream papers. If true, this would mean that one million British children are exposed to neglect, emotional harm or physical or sexual assault every year — a figure that is ten times higher than the annual number of cases investigated (Hope 2008). Some did question this claim, pointing out that such categories as 'emotional abuse' and 'neglect' suffer from a lack of clear definition and vary widely between nation states. But the fact that the 'one in ten' statistic was so casually bandied around indicates that there is a predisposition to see the worst in parents; an acceptance of the idea that perfectly ordinary families are a mere smack or shout away from child murder.

We know that this isn't the case — from the statistics, from our own experience of life, from the dozens of happy and healthy children we see running around school every morning. So why is the worst seen to be so believable?

This, in many ways, is the big question of this book, and is discussed over the following chapters. The view of parents as the villains of the piece results from a combination of a parenting culture that sets expectations of parents that are both unreasonably high, and insultingly low. This problem is compounded by a policy shift that presents parenting as the root cause of all evils and the solution to all social problems. Again, this rests on the contradictory expectation that parents can and should solve everything from crime to bad health to educational failure through practising particular parenting skills, whilst assuming that parents are too incompetent even to be trusted with such basics as talking to their children and loving them in the right way.

The key thing to note is the degree to which the politicisation of parenting is new. For more than a century, 'family breakdown' has been cited as both a cause and effect of society falling apart. But the focus upon parenting — the behaviour of individual parents and their relationship to their children — that dominates today's discussion has a sharper edge. Politicians and commentators do not moralise about the family in a direct way: rather, they are engaged in a process of moralisation that dare not speak its name, where moral concerns are presented as objective, scientific problems of children's health and happiness. Often, concerns are presented as coming from children themselves — as with the recent *Good Childhood Inquiry* commissioned by the Church of England Children's Society, which presented a host of traditional churchy complaints about the problem of working mothers, single parents, and individualistic values, but couched these as new 'findings' that came out of discussions with several thousand children (The Children's Society 2009a). In a similarly cowardly fashion, officials attempt to engage with parents through their children, engaging children as the messengers of the latest good parenting advice—which itself is based on bogus evidence and shameless scaremongering. So a multi-page leaflet produced for the Department of Health's 'Change 4 Life' campaign is brightly coloured and filled with puzzles and pictures for the kids, while it begins with the parent-oriented (and highly questionable) message:

> If things go on as they are, 9 out of 10 of our kids will grow up to have dangerous levels of fat in their bodies (DH 2008).

By hiding behind children, experts, and so-called evidence, the new moralisation of parenting presents itself as an unquestioned truth, and becomes quickly internalised in the everyday lives of parents. By spreading its remit beyond a concern about particular kinds of families or particularly troubled children to addressing a presumed problem with all families and all children, the scope of parenting intervention expands to embrace every aspect of life. And with the focus on 'parenting' to the exclusion of every other social or cultural development, parents find themselves quite simply blamed for everything.

Making an issue out of everyday life

Take the concern with children's behaviour, which dominates debates about everything from toddler-taming to education to youth justice. Are today's children more badly behaved than previous generations? The obvious answer is, yes. From the rapid increase in the number of Antisocial Behaviour Orders (ASBOs)— penalties issued by the civil courts to young people behaving badly on the streets—to the lack of discipline among school pupils to the daily traumas undergone by the families on *Supernanny* as a result of their children's tantrums, we seem to be surrounded with examples of children out of control and parents who cannot cope. Yet there is another side to all of these stories.

There has been a dramatic rise in the number of children with ASBOs because, until very recently, Anti-Social Behaviour Orders did not exist. Indeed as writer and former youth worker Dr Stuart Waiton has argued, even the concept of 'antisocial behaviour' is new: until the 1990s this term was rarely used, whereas now it is ubiquitous (Waiton 2006). Antisocial behaviour, argues Waiton, is used as a catch-all term to describe anything from noisy neighbours and graffiti to kids hanging out on the street: it amounts to 'criminalising mischief', labelling what used to be everyday, unremarkable teenage behaviour as an offence, to be recorded and presented as evidence of a national social problem. In other words: it is not that we are suffering from an epidemic of antisocial behaviour, but that teenage behaviour that, in more positive-spirited times, was accepted as on the margins of acceptability is now labelled as a crime. And where children's behaviour has become more problematic than in the past, it is far from clear that this is simply the result of 'poor parenting', rather than a more general reflection of a broader crisis of adult authority, which extends way beyond the home.

Any teachers' union—pretty much any teacher—will tell you at length how today's pupils are more badly behaved than previous cohorts, and the blame is invariably laid at the parents' door—they feed their children the wrong things, they discipline them in the wrong ways (if at all), they treat the school as an adversary rather than an ally. Yet we also know that the way schools discipline pupils has changed: that schools are more likely to exclude children; that teachers are increasingly worried about raising their voices to pupils or giving them bad grades because of the risk they might become a target of allegations of abuse, bullying or dented self-esteem. In 2006 an average of 1,700 pupils were excluded each school day. Parents are required to ensure that these pupils, on 'home detention', are supervised for the first five days, and they are fined £50 if they fail (BBC News Online 2007: 4 September). This is alongside the existing raft of penalties: parenting contracts for truancy and misbehaviour, parenting orders for serious misbehaviour in schools and penalty notices for truancy, all of which, in the words of the Department for Children, Schools and Families, were 'introduced as a balanced package of support and sanctions to reinforce parental responsibility for school attendance and behaviour' (DCSF 2009: Accessed 7 February).

Given the ongoing crisis of education that feeds daily headlines in the UK, we have to ask: How can all this be parents' fault? How has it come to be assumed that if children don't behave at school, this is down to problems with their behaviour at home, rather than the way the school is dealing with things? And how are parents supposed to cope with being blamed for every problem to do with their child when everything their child is or does can be labelled a problem?

From hanging out on the street (Antisocial Behaviour) to teasing in the playground (now defined as bullying), from running around too much (hyperactivity) to sitting too still and quiet (being sedentary), there is no aspect of a child's behaviour that somebody, somewhere, could not define as a problem. A friend of mine was called into her son's school for a 'chat' about his behaviour: apparently he asked and answered too many questions in class. Was he interrupting the teacher, or the other children? No. Was his behaviour disruptive, at all? No. But being a bright boy and keen to have his finger on the button meant that he seemed unwilling to hold back and let the other children have a go—a problem, the school suggested, with his 'listening skills'. The school suggested counselling; my friend moved house, in the hope that a rather better school wouldn't view being clever as a learning disability or a behavioural problem.

And it's not just behaviour. In Britain's war against childhood obesity, feeding one's children chicken nuggets or chocolate is seen as some form of abuse. Was it really only a few short years ago, in 2005, that celebrity chef Jamie Oliver launched his crusade against the British school meal? As Oliver waded in to transform the lives of school pupils by banning the unhealthy food that they would eat and laboriously producing all manner of 'healthy' food that they refused to touch with a barge pole, policymakers' obsession with children's diet and weight suddenly gained a new momentum. The content of school dinners became a defining issue of the 2005 General Election, with the mainstream parties falling over each other to pledge just how much money and effort they would expend on schools to improve the quality of nosh on offer during the 45-minute lunch break. (Forget the rest of the school day—who cares about the quality of maths, science or history?).

The spotlight centred, first, on school canteens and the cheap processed rubbish they were churning out every day: predictably, however, the focus of the debate became parents and the cheap, processed rubbish they were forcing down their children's throats *all the time*. 'How can we be held responsible for the bad eating habits children learn at home?' moaned the schools; and the lazy parent, hell-bent on ruining their kids with a diet of Turkey Twizzlers, fizzy drinks and chips, became the culinary *bête noir du jour*. So in the second series of *Jamie's School Dinners*, Oliver turned his fire on packed lunches—'the biggest evil'—and let rip about the source of that evil:

> I've spent two years being PC about parents. It's kind of time to
> say if you're giving very young kids bottles and bottles of fizzy
> drink you're a fucking arsehole, you're a tosser. If you've giving

bags of shitty sweets at that very young age, you're an idiot (Cited in Lyons 2006).

Oliver's extraordinary speech raised not an eyebrow in policy-making circles. Rather, the ravings of this sanctimonious cook, who clearly thinks that knowing how to cook a sea bass gives a unique insight into parenting skills, simply added a veneer of cool to policymakers' prescriptions. In September 2007, the School Food Trust—a body set up after the General Election of 2005 with £15 million in funding from the Department for Education and Skills 'to promote the education and health of children and young people by improving the quality of food supplied and consumed in schools'— issued a press release bemoaning the 'nutritional content' of packed lunches compared with school meals (School Food Trust 2007). Children now face a bewildering array of regulations about what should and should not be in their lunch box, and humiliating consequences if their parents have not complied. In the summer of 2007, I was interviewed by Radio Four's *Woman's Hour* on the question of whether there was too much government intervention into children's diets, and the item began with a case study of a mother Somewhere Up North, struggling with the daily tension between giving her children some nice lunch they would eat and complying with the rules laid down by the school. One day, this mother packed a chocolate chip muffin for her daughter. When her daughter reminded her that they weren't allowed anything with chocolate in it, the mother shrugged it off: 'Oh, just tell them it's raisins, they won't care'. Of course, the misdemeanour was discovered, the child humiliated, and the mother chastened. One can only imagine what might have happened if the child had been sent to school with some really 'evil' snack, like a can of Coke.

The advent of the Packed Lunch Police is a truly nasty moment in the relations between parents, schools, government officials and, of course, children. It presents parents as uncaring incompetents— 'arseholes', 'tossers'—who cannot be trusted with decisions about their children's daily diets; sets schools up to spy on them; and makes children the victims one way or another—of raw carrots if the parents comply, of ritual castigation if they do not. It also further elevates diet and food as a key part of schooling—which it really should not be. What matters about a school, surely, is not what children eat and drink, but what they learn and think.

The basis of this obsession with lunch boxes is the problem—nay, 'epidemic'—of childhood obesity. What is often ignored is the extent to which the scale and magnitude of this problem is contested. Children are getting chubbier, for sure—but that scarcely means that they are teetering on the brink of morbid obesity, illness and death. The relationship between diet, weight and health is a complex one—the relationship between diet, weight and health in childhood and that in later life is even more so (Luik, Basham and Gori 2006; Gard and Wright 2005; Campos 2004). Yet on the basis of an assumption that fatter children are going to die earlier and it's all their parents' fault, a whole new layer of official nagging and guilt-tripping has been brought into everyday life, making daily tasks like packing lunch boxes or cooking dinner into fraught exercises in toeing the line. Meanwhile, children are subjected to humiliating weigh-ins at school, and the idea that obese children should be taken away from their parents by Social Services is gaining increasing influence (Fitzpatrick 2008).

Discipline and healthy eating are only two examples of the way in which the minutiae of everyday life is now held up for scrutiny, against a cultural abuse-ometer that silently clocks up presumed parental failings against an increasingly dogmatic regime of acceptable appearance and behaviour. At a time when feeding chips to one's children, or allowing them to watch 'too many' hours of television, or administering a swift smack on the back of the legs, or failing to read the requisite number of bedtime stories, are genuinely considered to fall so far short of acceptable parenting that they lie on the spectrum of 'abuse', it is hardly surprising that we are confronted with statistics telling us that one-tenth of children are 'abused' by their parents, or that we are presented with ever-more bossy and shrill policy designed to promote 'Good Parenting', and punish that which falls short. What might seem more surprising is that we parents just sit there and take it. Why? Because we have somehow bought into the flip-side of parent-bashing: that we are victims as much as we are villains, and if we do wrong it is not our fault.

Chapter Three

Parents as Victims

If a politician were to do a Jamie, and stand up in Parliament proclaiming that 'parents are tossers' and that he, personally, knew better than everybody else about how to prepare the perfect family meal, some hackles would surely rise. If the burgeoning number of parenting support groups and social networks had as their moniker 'because parents are too stupid to follow instructions' rather than 'because instructions aren't included', they might find themselves rather less popular. But with the possible exception of teenage mothers, about whom, it appears, one can say anything, Those Who Know Best tend not to wear their contempt for parents on their sleeve.

Rather, parents are insulted in caring, therapeutic terms — we 'cannot cope' with the 'pressures of modern living'; we need 'advice and support' rather than blame and castigation; we are trying to do 'a difficult job' in a 'complex world'; and our 'social isolation' demands that we need more 'social networks' to be created for us. According to a government-sponsored report in 2007, it's not even really our fault that our kids are fat: we are merely the products of an 'obesogenic society', in need of collective help to get over our attachment to carbs and cars (DIUS 2007).

Parents today are treated as a problem: not as 'bad parents' wilfully screwing up their children's health and future, so much as hapless, helpless parents who know not what they do and need guidance about how to do it better. The problem of the modern parent is presented not as one of parents choosing to behave irresponsibly towards their children, but as parents being victims of a broader culture of irresponsibility, and therefore having no choice but to be bad parents — or at best, less-than-perfect parents. We are repeatedly reminded that the transition from footloose-and-fancy-free middle-youth to new parent is a massive shock to the system; that a new baby is a great deal to cope with; that many parents struggle with feelings of guilt and loneliness; that parenting is the 'most important job in the world' which, like a job, requires training and, like a job, is possible to fail at. That government officials try to link the need for parenting classes to the popularity of *Supernanny* is not at all surprising. In the official view, all parents are experiencing the degree of turmoil undergone by *Supernanny*'s participants, and the role of the state really is like a cuddly Jo Frost—not to blame, but to help, support and advise us onto the right path.

'Supporting Families'

Since the New Labour government was elected in 1997, family policy has been high on its agenda. The 1998 consultation document *Supporting Families* showed the shift in New Labour's thinking from that of previous governments, with its explicit concern that families could not simply be left alone and relied upon with the help of the odd tax break or there, but that they need to be actively supported by the state in an emotional kind of way (Home Office 1998). The foreword, by then Home Secretary Jack Straw, noted, first, that families are still important—'the foundation on which our communities, our society and our country are built'—but that they are 'under considerable stress'. He went on to acknowledge that families 'do not want to be lectured or hectored, least of all by politicians'—yet claimed that they *did* want a friendly kind of intervention by the state:

> [W]hat families—all families—have a right to expect from government is support. ... [They] want clear advice to be available when they need it on everything from their children's health to their own role as parents.

The idea of families expecting and wanting a friendly kind of support was the springboard for the therapeutic policy proposals laid out by *Supporting Families*—parenting classes, pre-marital counselling, and so on.

At the time this was reasonably controversial stuff: as one article in the *Guardian* mused, 'It's all very well being told how to bring up your children, but how do you feel about being forced into classes to learn how to do it properly?' (Segrave 1997). Critics muttered about the nanny state, and commentators pointed to the irony of being told how to parent by Jack Straw, whose teenage son had previously been cautioned for selling cannabis to an undercover reporter (Hope 2007). But while there were no great celebrations of New Labour's *Supporting Families* initiative, there was no rebellion either. The idea of the government teaching parents to parent was received as a bit cheap, a bit bossy, but an acceptable intervention in those rare cases where feckless, clueless parents were raising tearaway kids.

Seven years later, as part of the launch of the government's 'Respect' agenda to tackle antisocial behaviour, Tony Blair delivered a speech to parents in Watford, titled simply 'Speech on improving parenting' (Blair 2005). The slightly defensive tone of New Labour's 1998 document—the recognition that families 'do not want to be lectured or hectored, least of all by politicians'—was gone, replaced with a bullish argument as to why concerns with parents' liberty are no more than a silly indulgence:

> You know a few years ago probably the talk about sort of parenting orders and parenting classes and support for people as parents, it would have either seemed somewhat bizarre or dangerous, and indeed there are still people who see this, is this an aspect of the nanny state, or are we interfering with the rights of the individual. And I think the point is this, we need to give people that support, and we need to do that particularly in circumstances where if we don't give people that support, and also put pressure on them to face up to their responsibilities as a parent, they end up having an impact on the whole of their local community. So it is not something we can just say well that is just up to you as to whether you do this properly or don't do it properly, because unfortunately the way that you do it makes a difference to the lives of other people.

In 1998, the government promoted a softly-softly approach to telling families what to do, claiming that families merely want 'clear advice to be available when they need it'. By 2005, the carrot had hardened into a very definite stick. Through parenting orders, argued Blair, 'Parents themselves can be forced … to accept support and advice on how to bring discipline and rules to their child's life'. And while the government had to accept that some parents really did *not* want this kind of 'support', they were to be forced to accept them anyway for their own good:

> [W]hile most parents on these orders can resent them initially, I think often they grow to value the support they receive, and the vast majority indeed do comply with the order.

The speed at which the New Labour government's insistence that it just wanted to hold parents' hands morphed into a full-on defence of issuing parents with court orders and locking them up if they did not comply shows the danger of accepting politicians' pronouncements at face value. It also, however, shows how closely the touchy-feely therapeutic dynamic that casts parents as victims, doing a tough job in a difficult world, is related to heavy-handed law'n'order. On one hand, the authorities worry about parents being victims of an 'obesogenic' society and issue us with friendly, colour-ful advice about how to navigate our diets through that; on the other, fat kids end up on the child protection register.

The trouble is that it's not just the government that seeks to por-tray parents as victims who therefore need increasing amounts of advice and support. Parenting experts, who appear genuinely sym-pathetic to parents and their struggles in managing family life, rou-tinely reassure us that it is not our fault that we find things hard, and encourage us to seek official help and advice on everything from feeding to potty-training. Parenting groups, whether official ones like Parentline Plus or more homespun social networking organisa-tions like Mumsnet and Netmums, are constantly reaching out to stroke the parental brow, telling us that they understand and shar-ing with us stories of countless other parents suffering in just the same way. *Supernanny, House of Tiny Tearaways* and whatever reality parenting shows the future will bring, have at the heart of their programmes sympathy for the parent, and advice to make things easier. And it works because, let's face it, there is nothing more con-ducive to self-pity than new parenthood. It's hard work, it's lonely, it's often boring, and we are terrorised by the spectre of getting something wrong. We want sympathy; we often feel we want sup-port. The question is—do we want the kind of support that is offered, from the kind of agencies that offer it?

The rise of the parenting expert

One of the most significant changes between bringing up children today and a generation ago has been the meteoric rise of the parenting 'expert'. As Christina Hardyment argues in her reflection on the parenting debate in Part Two, there have always been advice manuals and people who think they know best about bringing up other people's kids. But the ubiquity, and variety, of the parenting expert today reflects a decisive shift in the power of the third party to inform individuals' attitudes and practices. We all know who these experts are: the voices of scientific and medical authority who write books and conduct research in their role as doctors of medicine, social science, or psychology; the pundits who write columns in mainstream newspapers as well as parenting magazines; or nannies like Jo Frost whose qualification is no more than having worked with children. Parenting experts can be anybody, it seems; providing they are not our friends, family members or ourselves. And we all know where the parenting experts are: in doctors' surgeries, self-help books, parenting magazines, newspaper pages, internet sites, reality TV. However much you try to avoid parenting advice, it is impossible to escape at least a fleeting knowledge of the latest fashionable toddler-taming method, or the sense of being vaguely inadequate in how you are raising your kids.

The dominance of the parenting 'expert' has been recognised as problematic—even by those who have played a significant role in shaping the genre. In 2007, pop-child-psychologist Tanya Byron, best known for her role as super-mentor in the tots-behaving-badly reality TV show *House of Tiny Tearaways*, launched an attack on her own industry. 'Parents are overwhelmed by advice and tips from an industry growing out of the most basic and instinctive aspect of life—child rearing', Byron wrote in the *Times* (London). She went on to confess:

> I have become part of this industry in writing books and making TV programmes about children and families with behavioural problems. However, as the success of the media-parenting industry grows, I find that the mothers and fathers whom I meet each week in my clinics seem more and more confused ... My belief is that the 'parenting industry' is marketing a simplified and unrealistic view of raising children, which is based on the notion that to be a parent is a series of problems to be solved and techniques to be mastered (Byron 2007).

I agree with every word Byron says—but I remain deeply suspicious about her reasons for saying it. Nobody who has suffered through an episode of *House of Tiny Tearaways* could believe that Byron genuinely thinks that parents know best, and should be left to get on with it. The fact that Byron turned on her own industry just in time to launch her own new child-rearing advice guide, called *Your Child ... Your Way*, suggests to me that her belief in parental 'empowerment' is partly PR. For example, some of her 'eight practical steps' to feeding your child 'your way' are packaged in fun language, but are nonetheless highly prescriptive about what parents should be doing and how they should be feeling about it. 'Chill out', says Byron, before instructing: 'Don't hover over your child or stare at them intently ... But still remain present if possible so that you are associated with the new calm environment'. Or how about this one: 'Have fun. Tell stories about the food; give them characters. Often telling a child that they mustn't eat and closing your eyes with lots of dramatic instructions not to eat will entice them to do it!' Even when those in the parenting industry recognise the extent to which endless advice-giving undermines parents' all-important capacity to trust in themselves and act with authority, it seems that the only solution is to provide yet more (if subtly different) advice.

Byron's about-turn came in the same month that it was revealed that the late Dr Benjamin Spock, the most famous and best-selling childcare guru of all time, had been plagued in later years by anxiety about the collapse of parental confidence, which he blamed largely on the parenting expert industry. 'What we've done with experts in parenting is to tell people that they don't know anything, and they have to rely on somebody that's done this and done that', Spock's widow, Mary Morgan, told Nancy McDermott:

> We undermine some of the greatest wisdom we've had handed to us: what we know intuitively. I'm not saying that the experts are wrong. I just think that this attitude has weakened the self-confidence of parents (McDermott 2007).

Indeed, the immortal line from Dr Spock—'Trust yourself. You know more than you think you do' (Spock & Parker 1999, p1)— seems to carry a greater irony the more the years elapse. Today's couples approach parenthood believing that they know nothing about it; and trusting yourself is a grand ambition indeed when you have been schooled in the idea that expert advice must be sought at every turn.

The diminishing of parental self-confidence, as Tanya Byron and Mary Morgan indicate, is not good for parents or children. But the advice persists, because it is based on a powerful idea: that the everyday practices of parenting, from what you feed the children to how you feed them, from how you get them to sleep to what method of discipline you use, matters fundamentally to the wellbeing of the child.

Madness in the methods

The idea that parenting practices really matter was controversially put to the test in the 2007 Channel 4 TV series *Bringing Up Baby*, a thinking-parents' reality TV series that combined the vogue for ever-more intrusive coverage of people's real-life experiences (in this case, life with a newborn baby) with a bit of history and analysis. The programme took six families with new babies, and assigned each one a 'mentor' who would guide them through the first three months according to a particular parenting style. The mentors were Claire Verity, a maternity nurse who represented the strict routine-based 'Truby King' method popular during the 1950s; Dreena Hamilton, representative of the indulgent 1960s 'do what you feel is best' method popularised by Dr Spock; and Claire Scott, who makes and sells baby slings and is a big fan of the 1970s 'Continuum Concept', whereby babies are always breast-fed, always sleep in their parents' bed, and are carried about everywhere with them. The mentors guided their charges through issues such as feeding, sleeping and generally living with their new babies, and had arguments with each other about breast-feeding in public and other baby-care methods of principle, while the occasional talking head popped up through the programme to add a bit of historical explanation.

Bringing Up Baby was fascinating stuff, not least because the series exposed childcare advice as something that changes over time. In setting out to test these changing fashions with real-life parents and babies, the series implicitly promoted the idea that it doesn't actually matter how you do it. And that proved really unpopular. Before too long, maternity nurse Claire Verity had become the pantomime villain, whose belief in leaving babies to cry led to her being spat at in public, issued with death threats, and told to stay away from the major London exhibition The Baby Show because the organisers feared a riot on their hands (Bennett 2007). The modern-day childcare guru Gina Ford, who is variously loved and loathed among mothers for her own advocacy of strict routines, wrote to the National Society for the Prevention of Cruelty to Children (NSPCC), to complain about the 'suffering of a tiny baby [being] used to sensationalise child-rearing methods in a television programme', and demanding that the NSPCC step in to stop 'production companies [continuing] this form of child abuse' (Hill 2007). Later, some doubt emerged over the veracity of Verity's formal childcare qualifications (*Daily Mail* 2007) — a claim that was leapt upon by her critics as proof that today's society would never condone, let alone accredit, the kind of 'abuse' that involves leaving a baby to cry.

Wherever you stand on the question of strict routines and newborn babies, there was something troubling about the passionate hatred aroused by Claire Verity. Partly, it was based on the idea that her methods really did amount to child abuse; that the babies concerned would suffer forever from the three hours in the garden that they experienced as a newborn (a concern that many rational people find pretty ridiculous). More significant, however, was that Verity simply refused to engage in the child-centred practices that, today, are really the only game in town. Her attitude that a baby should fit around a parent's life, rather than parents taking their cue from the infant, is so out of line with the demands of contemporary parenting culture that she was seen as deserving of a witch-hunt. And what everybody, from the most child-centred 'militant lactivist' to self-styled hardliners like Gina Ford, found most intolerable was the way that Verity's acceptance of bottle-feeding, babies sleeping in their own rooms and learning to adapt to routines set by their parents refused to endorse the orthodoxy of mother-baby 'bonding' over the first few weeks.

'Signal moments'

The US academic Rebecca Kukla, author of the excellent *Mass Hysteria: Medicine, Culture and Mothers' Bodies* (2005), has discussed the modern cult of intensive mothering in terms of an obsession with 'signal moments' in child-rearing—moments that stand as a series of tests about how good and devoted a mother is. '"Good" mothers are those who pass a series of tests—they avoid a caesarean during labour, they do not offer their child an artificial nipple during the first six months, they get their child into a proper preschool, and so on,' she argues. Furthermore, 'Mothers often internalise these measures and evaluate their own mothering in terms of them' (Kukla 2007).

This will be a familiar story to anybody who has had a newborn baby and tried desperately to do the 'right thing', as opposed to just the thing that might work. If you really believe, say, that having a natural childbirth will be very important for your baby, the sense of failure—and worry for your child's future—when you fail the test of this signal moment and demand an epidural is terrible. Or you might try really hard to feed your baby organic casseroles that you have made yourself, because you believe this will have a significant impact on their future health and abilities, only for the child to decide that he/she will only eat processed food out of jars. Having emotionally invested in doing the 'right thing' on the grounds that this will improve your child's chances, it becomes very difficult to think, when the right thing doesn't work out, that it doesn't really matter and the child will be fine.

An over-preoccupation with doing 'best for baby' has translated itself into a whole lot of guilt and fear about what happens if we fail at any point. This represents a thoroughly unhelpful myth that has been termed parental causality, or parental determinism: 'the notion that parental intervention determines the fate of a youngster' (Furedi 2001). On one hand, parental determinism portrays parents as gods, whose every action (cuddling, shouting, co-sleeping) will have a major impact upon their child; and on the other as incompetents, who are incapable of making the smallest decision without expert guidance, because all of these small decisions are seen as crucial signal moments.

The bonding myth

Mother-baby 'bonding', facilitated through breast-feeding and keeping the infant close to the mother's body as much as possible, is the most significant of these 'signal moments' — and any mother will be only too aware of the importance attached to this. Before the birth, you will be advised of the many benefits of breast-feeding over bot-tle-feeding, one of which is that breast-feeding will apparently help you to 'bond' better with your child. At the birth, the conscientious midwife will lay the baby on your naked breast, to ensure that you get some all-important 'skin-to-skin' contact and to help you to 'bond'. (If the slapdash midwife, or doctor, does not do this, you can be sure that the conscientious midwife later on will ask you whether you got the 'skin-to-skin', and if you say no her face will reveal that this is a grave problem, which will make your baby suffer terribly). On the postnatal ward, however exhausted and weak you may be from the labour, you will be sure to have your baby with you at all times next to your bed, as this helps you to bond better. If your baby has to spend some time in the Special Care Baby Unit, you may see that the baby's notes have a special section dedicated to 'bonding', in which it is logged how many times you came to the hospital, tele-phoned the hospital, cuddled the baby and so on. There is no doubt that bonding is a Big Deal.

Yet right back in the 1980s, research showed that, in fact, bonding is a Load of Rubbish. Or as the academic obstetrician William Ray Arney more politely puts it, 'Bonding theory, like much theory developed in obstetrics, has all the characteristics of a pseudo-science, "a sustained process of false persuasion transacted by simu-lation or distortion of scientific inquiry and hypothesis testing"' (Arney 1982, p169). Two American researchers, Marshall Klaus and John Kennell, published their landmark research into bonding in the mid-1970s, claiming to show that mothers' feelings towards their newborn infants could be scientifically measured in terms of how well they were 'bonding', and that better bonding led to better chil-dren. Over the course of the following decade, this piece of research was comprehensivelytra shed: a story that Diane Eyer tells in her superb critique *Mother-Infant Bonding: A Scientific Fiction* (1992). Yet despite being revealed as a 'scientific fiction', the bonding bandwagon carried on regardless, with everybody from the obstetrics profession to the natural childbirth movement to parenting experts to policymakers leaping on 'bonding' as the next solution to all of society's problems.

As Arney argued 20 years ago, 'Much of the research on bonding is methodologically flawed. Yet bonding theory has been accepted uncritically despite its demonstrable scientific problems' (Arney 1982, p156). Why? According to Arney, because focusing on the primacy of a mother and infant's physical and emotional attachment to one another provides a convenient way of boosting the 'prejudice' that 'women interested in pursuing a life in which children are not the *raison d'être* of women or their exclusive focus of attention' will damage their children as a result (Arney 1982, pp172–3). This is undoubtedly true, and given impetus by the present-day orthodoxy of child-centredness discussed in the next chapter. But the significance of bonding is not only that it reinforces the 'social order', of the natural mother stuck at home with the kids. It lays the most intimate, spontaneous, emotional aspect of parenthood open to scrutiny and intervention by professionals.

What does it mean for hospital staff to be standing around trying to assess how much you appear to love your new baby? When a midwife or breast-feeding counsellor spends hours by your side getting the baby to latch on properly so that you will love the baby more, what does this reveal about official views about parents? It is as though parenthood is considered so alien to us—even after nine months of pregnancy—that we cannot be trusted even to feel affection for the child, without oodles of interference by Those Who Know Better. This degrading view suggests a massive loss of faith in parents' basic humanity—let alone their particular parenting styles.

Regulating instinct

The obsession with 'bonding' and various other methods of managing parental emotions rests on the notion that we have to be taught by pseudoscientific experts how to love our children. It is not just that we have to turn to experts to find out exactly what to do with our children, in terms of how to discipline them or get them to sleep at night: now, we are considered in need of guidance about how we feel about them. The parent-child relationship is no longer seen as something special and personal that just exists, but as the determining force in a child's life that must be artificially created according to the dictates of Good Parenting.

A clear example of this concern about parental (and particularly, maternal) feelings about their children is given by the over-zealous attempts to root out suspected cases of Post-Natal Depression (PND) in new mothers, through getting them to check off statements from a list about how often they cry, feel sad, think that everything is their fault: unless the new mother claims to feel ecstatic about everything, she will be logged as a problem and firmly guided towards feeling the right kind of love for her child.

For many health professionals and new mums alike, it's a bit of a joke—in the maelstrom of new babyhood, everything makes you worry and cry, and there's nothing like having to answer a question-naire about your emotional state to raise anxiety levels. 'Did I pass?' I asked my health visitor after the birth of my second child. A rant published by 'Exhausted Alice' in the 'Bollocks of the Week' section on the Bad Mothers Club website (Bad Mothers Club 2009b) shows one new mother's frustration with the constant assumption that she was depressed rather than tired and fed up:

> What is all this bollocks about PND in any case? Pretty much any woman with a new baby causing sleeplessness who answers the Edinburgh Postnatal score truthfully would be defined as depressed, especially with all the 'advice' out there about how to do it properly! ... Of course I'm f***ing depressed—I have 2 small children and a small baby who won't let me sleep. If I got more sleep I wouldn't be 'depressed'. Do you have a pill for that? No, I didn't think so.

But the obsession with rooting out PND among new mothers is more than a passing fad. In *Abortion, Motherhood and Mental Health*, the sociologist Ellie Lee documents how the diagnostic category of PND has gradually expanded from relating to a small number of extreme cases of puerperal psychosis to encompassing an ever-wider range of feelings following the birth of a child: many of which, as 'Exhausted Alice' indicates, relate more to sleep-deprivation and the practical demands of new parenthood than to clinical depression (Lee 2003). Yet health professionals are under increasing pressure to diagnose women with this problem—and women themselves seem to be inviting this diagnosis in.

In the summer of 2007, the social networking site Netmums pub-lished the results of its online survey of 5,300 mothers (Netmums 2007). Published under the dispirited title 'A Mum's Life', the survey claimed to find the nation's mothers stressed-out, unhappy, and above all mentally ill—with over half of respondents having suffered, or *thinking that they had possibly suffered*, from postnatal illness. This dubious finding takes the normalisation of PND to its logical conclusion: if over half of mothers suffer from PND, mental illness following childbirth must be the norm rather than the exception. Or to put it another way – all mothers are mad, and in need of therapy. Of course, the fact that Netmums asked mothers, not just whether they had been diagnosed with PND, but whether they thought they had possibly suffered from it, inflated the findings beyond anything believable as to the true extent of PND. What is interesting, however, is the way that mothers need little encouragement to look back on their experience of new parenthood through a highly negative lens, to the point of terming it 'depression'; and that Netmums, by encouraging this trend, thinks it is helping us out.

Netmums clearly hoped to draw attention to some of the stresses of motherhood, and call upon the government for more resources. But in terms of helping parents, the PND button is the wrong one to push. As Netmums' own survey shows, parents do not relate well to health visitors – less than half of mums would turn to a health visitor for 'parenting' advice or support, and only 14% would talk to a health visitor if they were feeling 'down'. By contrast, 70% would turn to a friend for parenting support, and 62% for personal support. Surely this is a very positive finding, showing that mums are less 'lonely and isolated' than is often assumed, and that we don't really want or need any more official emotional monitoring and support.

On the other hand – we could do with a bit of practical help. When asked what caused them stress in their everyday lives, 68% of Netmums' respondents said 'Keeping on top of their housework' and 63% said 'Lack of time "for me"' – far greater proportions than reported problems with their relationship, or their children's behaviour. Having been through two stints of maternity leave, I have often thought that what would make a profound difference would be some help with the daily monotony of housework, or some childcare to enable you to sleep, go shopping, read a book. Yet in all the discussion about the need for government initiatives to help new mums bond with their babies, make friends, or be happy (things that official interventions could never achieve), nobody ever mentions the simple, practical things that would be easy to do – a babysitter instead of a health visitor, perhaps. Or a bit less ersatz sympathy, and somebody else making the tea.

Chapter Four

Parents v Children

> When I was writing [the first edition of] *Life After Birth* I rarely, if
> ever, read pieces about the negative aspects of new motherhood
> and how to cope with them. Now I am regularly telephoned by
> journalists writing features on various aspects of my book ... The
> success of *Life After Birth* proves that women want and need such
> help (Figes 2000, ppx–xi).

While Kate Figes perhaps overstates the claim that her gloomy 1998
manual about the 'turmoil' of new motherhood is single-handedly
responsible for shift in attitudes towards parenthood, it is true that
the openly-expressed ambivalence, even downright negativity,
about 'life after birth' is a recent thing. Whether it's popular non-
fiction like Stephanie Calman's *Confessions of a Bad Mother* (2005),
personal confessionals like Rachel Cusk's *A Life's Work* (2001), or
close-to-the-bone novels like Allison Pearson's *I Don't Know How She
Does It* (2003), the bookstores are filled with cultural expressions of
the frustrations of motherhood. Mothers moan about the mess, the
anxiety, the lack of time alone, the constant feeling that you're not up
to the standards laid down by experts and policy-wonks, the fact
that fathers get off lightly, that you can't trust nannies/nurseries/
teachers/doctors ... and if they'd only known what motherhood
would mean for them, they might have thought twice before
embarking on this unrewarding journey. When Lionel Shriver won
the prestigious Orange prize for *We Need To Talk About Kevin* (2005), a
harrowing novel about a mother's strained relationship with her
sociopathic, mass-murdering teenage son, mumsy journalists
greeted the prize as a vindication of a new openness about the everyday problem of struggling to love your own children—hardly the
point, you might have thought (Bristow 2005).

Raising children has always been hard work, both in a physical
and emotional sense. Parents have always had to provide for their
children, clean up after them, and worry about them. But the daily
grind of parenting did not used to spark the intensity of resentment

and anxiety that it does now. What is it about today's society that makes bringing up children so much harder to do?

A new life — or a life sentence?

On the face of it, the dramatic rise in living standards in the Western world, the invention of appliances such as washing machines, dishwashers, computers, vacuum cleaners, the availability and acceptability of contraception and abortion, the existence of a real network of professional childcare and the acceptance of mothers' employment seems to make the physical and financial job of parenting easier than ever. People choose when to have children and how many they should have; the worry about 'another mouth to feed' is far less pressing than it was for our grandparents' generation. Indeed, before the credit crunch hit, the big concern among the chattering classes was the supposed problem of families being able to afford *too much* stuff, creating a new generation of rampant mini-consumers, with families gorging themselves on cheap chickens.

The flipside of life being easier, however, is that the 'emotion work' that goes into raising a family is much greater than in the past, and imposes a different, but no less onerous, burden on today's parents. The phenomenon of 'intensive mothering' (Hays 1996) means that parents feel the need to be constantly on hand for their children, responsible for every one of their educational, entertainment, nutritional and emotional needs. In *Paranoid Parenting*, Frank Furedi (2001) examines the impact of risk consciousness into everyday family life, which has created a situation where children are not free to play outdoors or to play with each other without adult supervision, and where relationships between parents have become fraught with distrust. The outcome of this situation is that parents find themselves frantically busy — rushing between work and home, constantly tending to their children, and feeling like it all comes down to them.

So what's the story? It is ultimately impossible to declare that raising children is either easier or harder than it was in the past — because in recent decades, the goalposts have shifted by miles. In the recent past it was taken for granted that having children was something that most people would do, and that they would get on with the business of raising them. Now, it is neither taken for granted that people will have children nor be able to bring them up. People are counselled to think very carefully before they take the big step to start a family, and to modify their expectations and lifestyles accordingly. Unplanned parenthood—particularly to young women (disparagingly known as 'teenage mothers')—has become the big sin of our age. Once the baby is born, an army of experts and advisors hovers around to 'support' new parents and give them guidance in what to do. As the child grows up, parents are seen to be subject to intolerable pressures over their children's education, health, and behaviour, and it is sagely advised that the worries never end, even when the grown-up children (eventually) leave home. Parenthood is now perceived as a burden that lasts from pre-conception to the grave—and having a family is seen as a lifestyle that people opt into, rather than an expected part of life.

The presentation of parenting as an uptight individualistic enterprise has warped both people's experiences of family life, and discussions about family policy. Parenting is no longer seen as a relationship based on trust, affection and spontaneous interaction, but presented as a task that can be undertaken with varying degrees of success, under the watchful eye of policy-wonks and experts. The idea that 'your life completely changes' when you have a child has become widely accepted, as have extraordinarily rigid ideas about *how* exactly your life is supposed to change: putting your child first and yourself last, with your job somewhere in the middle and your partner somewhere behind that.

This cultural turn that marks parenthood out as a distinct challenge with its own peculiar set of rules and conventions is decisively new, and extremely divisive. It sets parents against children, parents against other parents, mothers against fathers and parents against non-parents. Above all, it informs an individual identity crisis that sets individual parents against themselves, encouraging them continually to challenge their own instincts and judgement.

Parents v children
Child-centredness and the 'selfish mother'

In an interview in the *Sunday Times* under the headline 'Why you shouldn't let your kids rule your life' (Britten 2008), the US academic Katie Roiphe describes how a friend recently bought her two-year-old a pair of squeaky trainers that make 'a noise that would drive any adult insane':

> The fact that the child wanted the trainers was, for my friend, enough of a justification for inflicting them on herself, her husband and her family. So her world is punctuated by an unbear-

able high-pitched squeaking. To me, this is a metaphor for our generation's philosophy of parenting.

Roiphe, who has a young daughter, goes on to criticise the way that today's orthodoxy of child-centric parenting demands that the presumed needs and wishes of children trump all adult sense of agency. She describes how 'people plan their weekends around what their children want to do, rather than having them experience life through their parents', to the extent that 'in some marriages I see, the kids end up as a substitute for adult relationships; the relationship between the parents becomes so much about the children that it gets in the way of adult intimacy'. She describes the boredom of the children's playground, yet the way that 'even fascinating and brilliant women' will turn dinner-party conversations around to the question of whether it is important to make your own baby food. And she suggests that, 30 years ago, things were very different:

> When I was growing up in the 1970s and 1980s, my parents would have parties and the children would run around the garden, staying up late and eating what they felt like — there was much less of a controlling atmosphere. Now, we try to control every aspect of our children's lives. We think we can create the perfect child by giving them the right music lessons or choosing the right pushchair. It is taboo that any conversation with another adult should take precedence over something going on with your child. When I was a child, children played, and I don't remember expecting my mother to give me her attention no matter what she was doing.

Of course, not everybody's childhood memories will be like Roiphe's. The phenomenon of parents (particularly mothers) gaining a significant sense of self through focusing on their children, and obsessing on the 'incredibly mundane topic' of the practicalities of child-rearing, is not new. What is new is not the attempt to assert control over children's lives, but the basis on which that control is justified. Whereas it used to be assumed that parents needed to assert control over the dynamics of their family life in order for the family as a whole to function, now it is demanded that parents assert control over themselves in order to meet fully the needs and desires of their children. 'Child-centred parenting' means that the antennae of the family are permanently attuned to the needs of the child ('the right music lessons') or to satisfying their wishes (a pair of squeaky trainers). Or as Joseph Epstein puts it, we are living under the tyranny of 'Kindergarchy', where '[c]hildren have gone from background to foreground figures in domestic life', and adults subsume themselves in the 'joyless', highly-pressurised—and ultimately unsuccessful—business of trying to raise 'perfect specimens' (Epstein 2008).

The birth of child-centredness

Both Roiphe and Epstein see a sharp contrast between the child-centred obsession of today and parenting practice a generation ago. But the philosophy of child-centredness has its roots in those comparatively sensible days of the 1970s. Penelope Leach's *Your Baby and Child* (1977), credited with giving birth to this trend, stood in opposition to advice that preached the importance of routine and discipline in raising a small child. For the child-centred advocates, babies and toddlers knew what was best for them, and the good parent was to feed them on demand and never let them cry. Bad parents, by contrast, ignored their child's tantrums, or told them what to do, or attempted to fit the child's wishes around their own. And Leach's philosophy has had a powerful impact. *Your Baby and Child* has sold over two million copies to date, and Leach remains a household name.

But at the time of first publication, this was just a book, to be taken or left along with several other, different childcare manuals. Nowadays, child-centredness has become the official orthodoxy, dictating the terms on which everything from daycare for toddlers to high schools should be run. It means presuming that children have needs, desires and interests that are directly opposed to those of their parents—and that it is the parents' duty, at every turn, to figure out what these are and strive to meet them, regardless of whatever else the parents might want or need to do. This was the central message promoted by the Church of England Children's Society's *Good Childhood Inquiry*, which complained that 'excessive individualism' has resulted in a generation of parents who are too selfish to raise happy children (Children's Society 2009a and 2009b). While a few commentators drew attention to the report's many flaws (Finkelstein 2009; Hill, Davies and Hinsliff 2009), the tenor of much of the media discussion was echoed in a breast-beating article by the writer and broadcaster Daisy Goodwin, in which she 'looks at her own loving family and finds even she could do better' (Goodwin 2009).

This notion that adults and children have conflicting needs is both artificial, and damaging. When the practical business of family life is properly considered, how is it even possible to draw such a distinction? Earning a wage, putting food on the table, going on holiday, saving money—none of these things are for the benefit of parents alone, or children alone: they are crucial to the operation of the family as a whole. As families, we pursue a winding, muddy path that is broadly in line with how we want our life as a family to be. There is no conflict of interest. But the child-centred ethos denies and distorts this reality, by demanding that these practicalities are justified with specific relation to the children—and consequently doubling the family workload and anxiety levels. So parents feel they should cook food that is good for the kids (even it means eating substandard fare themselves late at night), adopt 'flexible working practices' so they can spend at least a day a week at home (despite the potential impact on their salary levels and promotion opportunities), or put their savings into Government-sponsored Child Trust Funds, which only the child is able to access when he or she reaches adulthood—thereby locking away funds that could be used for family emergencies.

It is worth noting that, despite the tagline 'child-centredness', this philosophy does not result in a better life for children. In *Reclaiming Childhood* (2009), Helene Guldberg persuasively explains how the current desire to keep children safe, both at a physical and emotional level, has led to a micro-management of their activities and a stifling of their freedom to play that is stunting their ability to develop. The 'helicopter parents' who hover over their children and structure the whole life around what they genuinely believe to be in the best interests of their children are often castigated for being 'pushy parents', whose own selfish anxiety is stressing their children out—a trend sharply satirised in John O'Farrell's novel *May Contain Nuts* (2005). In 2008, researchers from Newcastle University warned that the pressure to create the 'ideal family', living up to the standards set by the child-centred orthodoxy, risked raising a generation of spoilt children. 'There are lots of different ways of "doing family"', educational psychologist Dr Liz Todd told the *Daily Mail*. 'If we were to realise this instead of worrying about whether we're a good parent or have a functional family, then life would be much easier'. She continued:

> Today's children, rather than being emotionally deprived, are often actually over-indulged, where both parents and children care too much. This can cause a chain reaction, where families become their own worst enemies. Any emotional distress can escalate to the point where they blame each other for any problems, blowing everyday exchanges out of proportion (*Daily Mail* 2008).

There is little doubt in my mind that the politicisation of the family, and the artificial ideal of 'child-centredness', creates a highly pressurised situation which can be unpleasant for parents and stifling for children. Even more worrying, however, is the impact that this idea of a fundamental conflict of interest between parents and children has on that relationship. The more the idea that there is a conflict of interest between parents and their children is promoted, the more it risks becoming a self-fulfilling prophecy. Once parents are schooled into thinking that they must be 'child-centred', the spontaneous decision-making of everyday family life becomes much more of a tortuous process, and all kinds of tensions come piling in. Caught between the guilt about not always putting their children 'first' and the demands of their partners, their work, and their own desires and ambitions, parents understandably start to kick against the selfless ideal, and to ask 'what about me?'. This compounds the notion of a parent/child divide, and the idea that family life can be sub-divided into 'children's time' and 'Me-time'.

Me-time

Over the past few years, there has been an apparent backlash to the orthodoxy of child-centredness, which takes the form of the argument: 'It's good to be selfish sometimes'. One-time career women who have turned raising their children into a full-time mission and ambition, and who are still reeling from the shock of finding it all quite stressful, frustrating and bloody hard work, start broadcasting the 'taboo-breaking' notion that the good parent is one who isn't afraid to take time out for herself. This becomes the justification for using childcare while they go out to work (which they disapprove of), allowing the kids to watch telly (which they really disapprove of), and leaving the children at the mercy of their grandparents for a few days while they jet off on a mini-break (which makes them deeply uncomfortable, but hey, something has got to give).

Just to be clear — there is nothing at all wrong with children being in daycare or watching telly, and mini-breaks for parents are a very good thing. Me-time is not about the simple act of taking a breather from life with the kids: it is a philosophy of self-obsession, which implies that you are only 'you' when you have put the children on one side in a carefully-compartmentalised fashion. The pursuit of 'Me-time' is conceived of as a therapeutic endeavour, designed to make us into better parents and partners by re-connecting us with our Selves. 'When we go away, we become ourselves again and we remember who we are', says Honor Rhodes, director of development at the National Family and Parenting Institute. 'The adult relationship can run out of petrol, like any tank. When we recharge our batteries, we have something different, new and exciting to give to our partners' (Kavanagh 2008).

In this sense, Me-time is the flipside of child-centredness. It, too, rests on the notion that there is a conflict of interest between parent and child, and demands that this conflict be addressed by taking sides with the beleaguered adult against a tyrannical tot. Just as child-centredness implies that parents are self-centred individuals who need to learn to think of their children more than themselves, Me-time implies that parenting is a selfless and unrewarding activity that should allow mothers and fathers (but especially mothers) time off for good behaviour. But is that really what parenting is all about?

The reality is that having children has never been a selfless activity, and in an age of women's equality and contraception, it is surely even less so. People do not decide to have children for the greater good of the world in general—they have them because they want them. While the philosophy of Me-time focuses on what is lost to the individual by having kids—the ability to go out, to focus on one's career, to be carefree and spontaneous and badly behaved—it ignores the deeper question of what is gained. When individuals become parents they don't subsume themselves but extend themselves—in a sense, they become more than what they were before. The act of raising children, loving them, caring for them, setting them on a trajectory through life, is an act of selfhood, and people do it because they sense it is ultimately more rewarding and meaningful than the accomplishments they might make on their own, as individuals. As one mother put it to me in an email, explaining why she had recently withdrawn from studying full-time at university 'for a variety of reasons to do with the workload inherent in having both adults working 50 hour weeks with no backup childcare for when our two-year-old got ill':

> I've either been told that it's a terrible shame that the child is 'stopping' me from doing what I want to do, or that I'm a terrible mother for wanting to be at university in the first place. Neither is true: as a FAMILY we have things we want to do, a lifestyle we'd like to have, and we make the best decisions we can about how to get there for all of us. Life isn't a constant battle between what I want and my partner wants or what we want and what our child

wants (although my judgement is out on the 5am versus 7am getting up time battle!).

Like child-centredness, the promotion of the Good-to-be-Selfish-Sometimes Parent is damaging to the core relationships of family life. It assumes a fundamental conflict between adult and child, and foments resentment about the basic aspects of being a parent — that it's hard work, that it's for life, that there is no off button or instruction manual. Also like child-centredness, Me-time rests on an infantilised notion of the parent. Child-centredness denies the reality that adults should make decisions based on their instincts and experiences, and counsels instead that they should take their cue from the child. Me-time denies the reality that being a parent is a constant emotional and practical relationship, and counsels people to throw tantrums about their desire to escape.

Infantilising parents

The infantilising dynamic behind today's orthodoxy of child-centredness was commented upon by the columnist Rachel Johnson, writing about Wendy Brown, the 34-year-old mother in Wisconsin, USA, who 'pinched her 15-year-old daughter's identity, enrolled in high school and tried to join the cheerleading squad' because she 'wanted to be in exactly the same place, developmentally, as her own daughter' (Johnson 2009). Johnson adds to this everyday examples from London, including the existence of a 'Parent & Toddler Nursery' and the way that parents are expected to sit in on their children's music lessons at school, attend rehearsals and 'go to sessions at school to be instructed on how to "support" their child's learning at home'. Noting that even Barack Obama, president of the USA, is playing the same game through penning open letters to his children about how it was they who inspired him to run for president (Obama 2009), Johnson worries about parents who seem to be 'dispensing entirely with the important demarcation between parent and offspring, responsible adult and dependent child, and simply living as if the generations are fused together'.

The erosion of the cultural distinction between adults and children is a broader development, which has been commented upon in relation to areas of life other than parenting. From the cult of youth that encourages people to look and act like teenagers well into middle age, to the increasing phenomenon of grown-up children being reluctant to leave home — or the 'Boomerang Kids', who leave and then come back again — examples abound of the way in which

Noughties society is increasingly uncomfortable with the role of the grown-up. But while it is easy enough for a childless thirty-something to perpetuate the fashion and fantasy of eternal youth, it is a much bigger deal when parents start doing it too. Child-rearing is not rocket science, but it does require that those who bring up children recognise themselves as adults and are able to exercise authority in this way. That is one reason why, historically, the fitness of young teenage mothers to be parents has been questioned: summed up in the pursed-lipped disdain for 'children having children'. But, as Johnson's argument brings out so well, today the parents who are prone to 'dispensing entirely with the important demarcation between … responsible adult and dependent child' are not the frowned-upon teenage mums, but the intensive, child-centred parents who believe that they are doing the best for their children by living every moment of their childhood by their side—and whose belief in this is supported by culture and policy.

Of course, given that parents are not eight-year-old children who are grabbed by the plotlines in their children's books or likely to gain from the music lessons they attend, the everyday business of intensive parenting soon becomes frustrating, and intensely isolating. The diatribes that fill online 'mummy-group' discussion forums, the birth of the cocktail playgroup, the endless quest for Me-time—all these markers of contemporary mommy-culture reflect something of the pall that is cast by the orthodoxy of intensive parenting over parents' experiences of family life. But so individualised and divisive is this culture that parents find themselves cut off from the very people who might best be able to share the load—other parents.

Chapter Five

Parents v Parents

> I love being a mother, and now that I am experiencing the joys of
> female friendship, I love being a woman. I love the way that you
> can share anything and everything with your girlfriends, that
> you are not judged but accepted for who you are. ... And yet,
> despite the support we give one another, it has been a shock to
> discover that raising a child is the one area in which women are
> absolutely not supportive of one another, not unless you find
> kindred spirits who agree wholeheartedly with your philoso-
> phy, whatever your philosophy may be (Green 2004, p234).

Jane Green's novel *The Other Woman* (2004) is a tale about the
mother-in-law from hell, told through the character of a rather neu-
rotic new mum. Though Green's best selling novels would not rank
highly on any literary register, her blunt statements about life-as-
it-is-for-women-like-herself provide a useful barometer of the inse-
curities of middle-class thirty-something women in the Noughties.
Life Swap (2005) muses about the lives of rich and desperate housewives in American suburbia; *Babyville* (2001) uses three narrators to
discuss the various frustrations of unplanned pregnancy, problems
with conceiving, and stay-at-home motherhood. In all three novels,
a recurrent theme is maternal competitiveness—the idea that the
kind of mother you are is crucial to your identity, and that this
pushes women to adopt child-rearing attitudes and practices that
have more to do with their interaction with their peer group than
anything to do with their child.

The bitter divisions between mothers sparked by competing 'philosophies' of child-rearing will not be news to any modern parent.
Whether you insist on organic food for your children, whether you
allow them to watch TV (and how much), the degree of outdoor
independence you give them, whether you had a 'natural' birth ...
All have become touchy subjects, around which maternal friendships can be made and broken. The politicisation of parenting, with
its in-built assumption that every little thing that you do as a parent

Really Matters, has fuelled this identity war, taking it to ridiculous (yet no less destructive) heights. As Dani Garavelli writes in *Scotland on Sunday*:

> [W]here once the very act of giving birth gave mothers an unspoken sense of sisterhood, the atmosphere these days is far from the supportive chumminess of a traditional mums'n'toddlers coffee morning. Instead mothers square up to each other with the ferocity of pit bull terriers: alpha mummies versus beta mummies; yummy mummies versus slummy mummies; breast-is-best-ers versus bottle feeders; Penelope Leach-ists versus Gina Ford-ists (Garavelli 2007).

The endless maternal identities on offer have one striking thing in common: whatever identity you choose, it is All About You—what you want for yourself, your life, your kids. In today's mummy culture, the ebb and flow of family life doesn't really figure. Motherhood is transformed into an individual consumer experience, where you decide what you think it should all be about and hone your personality, friendship circle and nursery equipment accordingly. It's like having a birth plan that begins with conception and lasts forever. And, as with birth plans, even the most painstaking identity work tends to get messed up by real life.

In response to an article of mine discussing the question of home birth, I received an email from a mother in the USA. This mother, who is 'very active in the natural birth community' in Michigan and tried to have a home birth, told me how shocked she was at the reaction of her peers 'to *my* non-traumatised reaction to my own caesarean births'. 'The women in my group felt so sorry for my "horrible" births and expected me to be overcome with grief', she wrote:

> I felt the opposite! I was relieved that I didn't die in childbirth due to modern science. I was thankful for my two healthy children. They will always be perfect births to me.

This is a salient example of the gap that exists between the identities we construct, and how real life makes us feel and behave.

The identity game is one that everybody plays, yet which nobody will defend. From novels to journalism, from internet discussion boards to school-gate socialising, parents laugh with each other about how daft it is to make judgements about other parents based on which brand of yogurt they buy for their kids. Unfortunately, the petty lifestyle squabbles of the 'Mommy Wars' are only the manifestation of a deeper tension to do with women's role in society. Even in an era when women's equality is taken for granted, and women's employment is accepted both as possible and desirable, there remains a fundamental confusion about where mothers' talents and responsibilities lie.

The 'mommy wars' and the new maternal identity crisis

In *The Mommy Myth*, US academics Susan J Douglas and Meredith W Michaels (2004) hark back fondly to a world where housewives demanded wages, working mothers demanded daycare centres with dry-cleaners attached, and everybody recognised that simply having children was not a route to fulfilment. They wonder whatever happened to feminism, socialism, and to the notion that there must be other ways of treating women and raising children than the paltry choice between full-on privatised motherhood and the guilty work–family balancing on offer in society today.

The confusion expressed by Douglas and Michaels about why today's ambitious woman sees baby-making as her sole *raison d'être* is a reflection of the fact that this 'new momism' is the result of a number of different and contradictory trends. Nobody now promotes the idea, as they did in Betty Friedan's day of the *Feminine Mystique*, that perfect housewifery is a positive ambition: indeed, the Hollywood success that greeted Sam Mendes' film of the bleak 1961 novel *Revolutionary Road* indicates how tarnished that 'Golden Age' has become (Friedan 1963; Yates 1961). From cradle to college, women are taught about the importance of preserving individual identity and the pitfalls of staying home with the kids. But nor is there any sense, any more, that women can 'have it all' — the career, the kids, the lifestyle. When it comes to the tension between the public world of work and the private world of the family, the word of the decade is 'juggling'.

Working, and juggling

When Rachida Dati, the French Justice Minister, returned to work five days after giving birth to her baby by Caesarean section, her decision sparked an international outcry. Dati was attacked for neglecting her child (by failing to spend the all-important few days 'bonding'), for risking her health after a major operation (although medics think nothing these days of discharging women who have had C-sections to return to running the family home after a couple of days bed-rest), and above all for betraying other women, by encouraging the idea that birth is no big deal, and that employers should not have to provide lengthy periods of maternity leave. The vitriol spat out by the commentators—many of whom are working mothers themselves—showed the degree of intolerance there is for women who are up-front about taking their job as seriously as their kids. When Dati was subsequently forced to quit the French Government after reportedly falling out of favour with President Sarkozy, a somewhat shamefaced commentary by Lesley Thomas in the *Times* (London) admitted:

> Though many of us thought that she was a hormone-free alien species in slingbacks, it turns out that Dati might simply have been trying to save her job (Thomas 2009).

Whatever Dati's motivations for her swift return to work, the reaction to her decision indicated that hers was a lesson in how not to behave as a working mother. The only acceptable cultural script, it seems, is the one that is currently being polished by Michelle Obama, First Lady of the USA. Shortly after the election of President Barack Obama in 2008, his wife penned a cloying article for *US News & World Report* that sought to dampen any critical commentary about how the lives of the couple's young daughters might be blighted by having busy, famous and important parents:

> [E]ven as First Lady, my No 1 job is still to be Mom. At 7 and 10, our daughters are young. My first priority will be to ensure they stay grounded and healthy, with normal childhoods—including homework, chores, dance, and soccer (Obama 2008).

Making clear that her first priority lies, not with helping to run the most powerful country in the world but ensuring that 'my girls' can still have sleep overs, was clearly an attempt to appease those who believe that motherhood is destiny, and that destiny is full-time devotion to one's children. No doubt Obama had learnt from the experience of Sarah Palin, the running-mate of the Republican candidate, how *not* to express her commitment to politics above all. Even feminist commentators had vilified Palin, a mother of five, for the fact that she used childcare and had taken short maternity leaves to enable her to get back to pursuing her career (Furedi 2008).

Michelle Obama has presumably also learnt from the experience of Cherie Blair, professional barrister, mother-of-four, and wife of the former UK prime minister. Cherie Blair's time as a Downing Street wife, recounted in embarrassingly intimate detail in her auto-biography *Speaking For Myself* (2008), represented an interesting moment in the UK's acceptance of the professional, ambitious working mother, and the continuing cultural suspicion that attaches to any woman who is prepared to pursue her ambitions beyond the confines of her duties of a wife and mother. When, back in 2002, Cherie Blair became embroiled with a conman in an ill-advised property purchase in Bristol, she tried to excuse herself by complaining about how hard it is for working mothers to 'juggle' the demands of work, family and (in her case) government life (*Independent* 2004). The glee with which the British media slapped her down both for the error and the excuse went beyond even the forced righteousness of these sleaze-busting times. This was seen as an admission that indeed, women cannot have it all — and if they try to juggle, they will only end up dropping something.

Outside of the rarified world of first ladies and people in governmental office, the acceptance that women, once they are mothers, have a moral duty to eschew taking their jobs seriously in order to play a significant role in hands-on parenting, is encapsulated in the concept of 'work-life balance'. From extended maternity leave and the 'right to request flexible working' to the obsessive desire to get fathers to play a greater role in hands-on childcare, the acceptable way of discussing how to manage child rearing and working motherhood today is to talk about the guilt and stress of spreading oneself between work and 'life', and to limit one's career ambitions in order to 'be there' for your children.

It has been noted that, in the UK, the number of women occupying top jobs appears to be dwindling. Research for the *Sunday Times* in September 2008 found that over the past two years, the number of mid-sized companies among the top 100 where at least a third of senior managers are female has dropped from 40 to 31. In discussing the possible causes of this trend, columnist Margarette Driscoll wonders whether the problem is continuing discrimination against women, particularly once they have children — or whether in fact women are actively choosing not to engage with demanding, traditional top jobs in order to become 'mum-trepreneurs', creating the kind of work that can be 'woven around their families' (Driscoll 2008). In other words, whether women are dealing with the tough realities of expensive, inflexible childcare and a parenting culture that makes them feel guilty for leaving the home by simply opting out of the rat race and into a cottage industry — in much the same way that Kate Reddy, the burnt-out protagonist of Allison Pearson's cult novel *I Don't Know How She Does It*, ultimately chose to 'do it' (Pearson 2003).

Mum-trepreneurs, thrusting boardroom executives, part-time checkout staff, freelance journalists, teachers — how working mothers choose to balance their career with their childcare responsibilities is generally a personal, pragmatic decision, and there is no single, or right, way for individuals to engage with this challenging dilemma. What is disturbing, however, is the degree of negativity about work that informs the discussion about 'work-life balance'. We are no longer in the days where it was seen as morally unacceptable for mothers of young children to work: indeed, as single mothers on welfare benefits have found, official policy is more than keen to get them into jobs. What is morally unacceptable today, however, is for women to appear to devote themselves to their work more than, or as much as, to their children — by going back to work less than six months after their baby's birth, working longish hours or a five-day week, attending international conferences rather than Nativity plays. The idea seems to be that it is good to be a working mother, provided that you don't like your job too much and that you wear your guilt about the nanny/nursery/child minder on your sleeve.

This negativity of work, particularly ambitious work, inspired American *Vanity Fair* journalist Leslie Bennetts to write the bluntly-titled book: *The Feminine Mistake: Are we giving up too much?* (Bennetts 2007). *The Feminine Mistake* admirably attempts to put the positive case for why women should retain their position on the career ladder, and not give it all up to stay home with the kids. Unfortunately, much of Bennetts' argument rests on the rather depressing thesis that the odds are that your well-heeled husband will leave you someday; that he is more likely to leave you if you don't have a job; and that when he does leave you will be strapped for cash and unable to regain your former earning power. Bennetts' model of how ambitious women can 'have it all', meanwhile, seems to be based on her own experience of writing columns sitting in the car at soccer matches, and so on — fine for a secure and influential journalist, but a rather harder path for a nurse, teacher, team manager or CEO to follow.

A more convincing case for working motherhood was put by *Times* columnist Janice Turner, entering the great Rachida Dati row:

> Work is good, it can even be noble. It can make us forget ourselves. That is what we should tell our daughters. It can be hard, thankless, scary, joyless at times. But you will feel useful, purposeful, part of the world. Babies are meant to fit around our lives. We are the only generation in any culture to think the opposite (Turner 2009).

The idea that child-centred parenting has led women to re-think the importance of their career ambitions is generally treated as a positive step forward—as the cutesy moniker of 'work-life balance' would have it. But as Turner indicates, while these two trends certainly go together, it is far from evident that the upshot is progressive. In fact, both the obsessive character of parenting and the negativity about work represents a level of disenchantment with both arenas of life.

'Involving fathers'

Because the battleground of the 'mommy wars' tends to be working motherhood, and because mothers tend to be the ones practically engaged with intensively parenting their children, it is often assumed that the competitiveness between parents is really just a scrap between mothers. But it is important to note the extent to which the obsession with parenting, the negativity about work, and the practical difficulties involved in managing a family and two full-time jobs impact upon fathers too. In the resentment bubbling beneath the Jane Green-style 'mummy lit', the father of the child always comes in for a drubbing for his incompetence at looking after the child, his failure to unload the dishwasher, his slothfulness in reminding his wife that she is still beautiful, his unreasonable expectation that he should work a full week ... While female authors occasionally attempt to address the confusion experienced by the displaced dad, who doesn't know how to do right for doing wrong, there is a general assumption that women are the major victims of the piece, and that in a fair world fathers would be made to share the pain.

This mummy-centric view has some justification. Mothers are the ones who have to give birth and take time out of work; they tend to do more domestic work than men; they are arguably more affected by the defensiveness wrought by our child-centred culture when it comes to going to work, or wanting to achieve something for themselves (Hochschild 2003). But it would be wrong to assume that fathers are immune from these trends. Men may do less domestic work than women, but that does not mean a return to the 1950s: the expectation is there that they should do some of it, and that whatever they do will never be enough. The ongoing discussions about the possibility of shared 'maternity leave', so that men can spend quality time with their newborns too; the need for fathers to be able to take advantage of 'flexible working practices' so that they can help out on childcare; the philosophy of 'equally shared parenting' ... All of these trends are putting fathers under pressure to justify themselves as, not just Dads, but 'involved' Dads (Hardyment 2007; Collier and Sheldon 2008). To the degree that, in November 2008, the government launched 'a campaign to dispel the myth that dads are the "invisible parent", and presented research showing that 'public, health and family services across the board need to go much further in recognising and working with fathers' (DCSF 2008: 13 November).

All working mothers have probably been in the position of railing against the injustice of it all, and holding furious rows with their partner over the need to do the washing/be in for the children's bedtime/look after the kids while the mother goes out. There is no denying that working motherhood brings a set of practical tensions into the relationship between mothers and fathers, and that these are not easy to resolve. But it is worth asking whether the ad hoc, personal resolutions to these rows amount to anything approaching a solution to the issues of childcare and working motherhood. In many respects, the demand for fathers to become more 'involved' in the day-to-day caring for their children seems likely to result in more practical difficulties, and greater tensions between couples.

In launching the government's 2008 'Think Fathers' campaign, Children's Minister Beverley Hughes said that the campaign's intention was to:

> [B]ring home the messages to families, public services and the voluntary services that parental responsibilities should be shared equally among parents and we can reverse the outdated and out of touch assumption that dads are a bolt-on family accessory—nice to have but not essential (DCSF 2008: 13 November).

It is worth asking who, exactly, thinks of dads as a 'bolt-on family accessory'? Presumably not women who live with their partners, children, or fathers themselves. Hughes' typically dismissive turn of phrase reveals the extent to which a father's traditional role in providing for his family, playing with the children, and acting as a source of love and support for the mother, is now completely downplayed. As Richard Collier and Sally Sheldon note in their compelling study of 'Fragmenting Fatherhood':

> [P]aid employment and the 'breadwinner ethic' still remain of central significance in the formation of a distinct masculine identity for many men, and ... not just fathers, but also other family members, perceive being a 'good father' as something bound up with the role of breadwinner (Collier and Sheldon 2008, p130).

Yet from the viewpoint of today's policymaker, the idea seems to be that you are only a 'proper' dad if you are prepared to immerse yourself fully in the mundane practicalities of intensive parenting; that your role is only worthwhile if you act like we currently expect mothers to act. In this way, the negativity about work that affects working mothers also comes out in the discussion about fatherhood, as though the only opportunity fathers have to realise their ambitions and create their identities are through their children. But if we imagine the consequences of putting this idea into practice, the prospect for families is bleak.

Working mothers know that the price paid for maternity leave and 'flexible' working practices is a reduction in pay and promotion opportunities. So fathers guilt-tripped into taking these options find that their families have to bear the financial consequences. More to the point, mothers know that what makes life with small children so frustrating sometimes is the endless grind of daily tasks, the sense of never getting out, and the pitching of one's horizons at the level of the four walls of the house. If fathers, through their 'equal sharing' of parental responsibilities, are forced to adopt the same experience, what respite does anybody in the family have? In Wendy Walker's novel *Four Wives*, another riff on rich and desperate housewives in the US suburbs, working mother Marie is complaining to a friend's mother about her husband's failure to share domestic tasks. When the friend's mother asks, 'wouldn't that be awfully boring?':

> For a moment Marie pictured the version of Anthony her demands implied. Coming home from work, hanging up his keys on the right hook. Helping with dinner, engaging in the conversation as they ate. Clearing dishes, wiping the table. His small but growing gut hanging out of his pants as he got down on all fours with a wet sponge to clear the food from the floor. Then sorting whites from colours, pre-spotting stains on Olivia's sun dresses. The image was almost absurd, and it made her wonder. Is that what would bring it back — the desire to climb into bed at night and wrap her arms around him when he was still awake? (Walker 2008, p116).

As government-sponsored 'support services' organise themselves to create a direct line to Dad, the father's role as a back-stop of common sense against the craziness of official advice is undermined. How many mothers have come home in tears after a ticking-off from the health visitor or an irritating interview with a teacher to find themselves comforted by their partner stoutly proclaiming 'They're talking rubbish'? This position is only possible to adopt because, as yet, fathers are not subject to the daily irrationalities of expert parenting advice, and they are able to reflect with some distance on the everyday dramas and dilemmas of parenting that often threaten to overwhelm the primary carer. '[R]esearch suggests fathers' take-up of support continues to be limited', note Collier and Sheldon. 'Many fathers do not see *themselves*, indeed, as in need of support' (Collier and Sheldon 2008, p135). And this, I would argue, is an extremely good thing.

The frustration with feeling like you do it all, and the desire to get one's partner to share the load, is common to all mothers—and particularly acute when both parents work full time. But ultimately, seeking to involving fathers in equally shared parenting is no solution to anything. What we need are ways of disengaging both mothers and fathers from the overheated culture of intensive parenting, to free them up to pursue adult ambitions and to enjoy family life.

The case for childcare

The mommy wars are phoney. It is not that career moms really blame stay-home moms for their guilt, or vice versa. Rather, these arguments highlight the cultural ambivalence that currently surrounds family life. At a time when neither the public world not the private sphere can be expected to yield satisfaction, individuals are expected to juggle the demands of both. The official expectation is that this will lead to well-rounded individuals who have a connection with society both through the world of work and their role as a family. In reality, it leads to an intense sense of individual frustration, as individuals feel thwarted by their own lives and threatened by the lives apparently led by those around them.

The orthodoxy of child-centred parenting discussed in the previous chapter thwarts parents' ability to find satisfaction either at home or work. Those who believe they are doing what is best for their children by completely subsuming themselves into raising their children find themselves exposed on a hourly basis to the sense of anxiety that they are not doing things right, or right enough, and disproportionately unsettled by the competitive behaviour of other parents. Those who try to pursue their full-time career have the sense of fulfilment blunted by the expectation that they are really neglecting their children, and should be spending less time at the office and more time on hands-on tasks like wiping bottoms and preparing food. Those who attempt to balance it all by working that bit less so they can spend 'quality time' with their kids find themselves torn between two worlds, feeling like a skiver at work and an absent parent at home. And for what? Does any of this angst or guilt really make things better for children?

Beneath much of the angst about the working mother lies the age-old prejudice that children are somehow damaged by being looked after by anybody but their mother. Much of this concern is related to the bonding myth discussed in chapter three, and emanates, not from sound research into the actual outcomes for children who have been looked after by a nursery/child minder/nanny, but a fear that mothers who choose to leave their children in the care of another lack the appropriate kind of love for their children. I have to say that this is one of the few aspects of contemporary culture to which I have been relatively immune: my children both attended nursery full-time from when they were a few months old, and it has never occurred to me that the care and affection provided to them by the staff, alongside the fun they had with other children, was anything but a bonus. But I am continually struck by the level of anxiety that parents feel by the idea of nurseries, or other forms of paid-for childcare, which largely seems to be born out of the idea that they are somehow 'cheating' in the whole parenting game. And when surveys come out, as they invariably do, postulating that social forms of childcare make children more miserable or aggressive, the working parent sinks yet further into guilt and despondency.

So it was with some relief that I read Penelope Leach — the guru of child-centred parenting — launch a scathing attack on UNICEF for issuing a report suggesting that children who spend too long in formal childcare at too young an age may suffer from long-term — if small — effects, including 'behavioural problems, aggression, antisocial behaviour, depression and an inability to concentrate' (UNICEF 2008; Frean 2008). The report suggests that 'government policies on maternity leave and childcare provision could be at odds with "today's knowledge of the critical developmental needs of the very young child"' — which tells us, apparently, that babies need exclusively one-to-one care in the first year of life (Frean 2008). Noting that '[o]ne thing you can be sure of when childcare is the subject of debate is that reason goes out of the window', Leach provides a useful reality check. Historically, all kinds of family members and others have looked after children; large families have meant that one-on-one care was never the norm anyway; a lot of mothers don't work full-time and many babies are not in nursery full-time, but often cared for by grandmothers for some days of the week; there is conflicting evidence about the impact of nursery care on children's levels of happiness and co-operation; happy mothers make happy children, and so on. Leach concludes, in spirited fashion: 'Let's just remember: love isn't 24/7 or nothing' (Leach 2008).

There are numerous problems with current childcare provision in the UK: the most significant of which, in my view, are the shortage of places and the expense. With the typical cost of a full-time nursery place for a child under two standing at over £8500 per year in England, paying for childcare remains a significant stretch for working parents (Daycare Trust 2009). But part of the reason why childcare solutions are priced out of many parents' reach is because of the continued, ill-founded negativity about nursery care, which pushes parents to make particular decisions about work that are not necessarily the choices they would otherwise have made, and fashion for themselves a parenting 'identity' that they would not necessarily have chosen. This increases the tensions within and between families, as the one obvious policy measure that could help busy parents—a social system of childcare—is superseded by the anxiety-inducing flim-flam about 'juggling' and 'work-life balance'. Worse still, the UK's cultural reluctance to embrace childcare strategies fuels one of the most disturbing trends of our time—the fear of other adults having contact with our kids.

Chapter Six

Parents v 'Strangers'

No Kids: 40 Reasons Not To Have Children is the blunt title of a book by French controversialist Corinne Maier, published in the summer of 2007 to great attention in the UK press. Many of Maeir's '40 reasons' are the predictable individual lifestyle complaints about how much kids cramp the style we used to have when younger, free and child-less. 'You will struggle to continue having fun yourself', Maier tells us. 'You will lose touch with your friends. Your children will kill your desire. Children sound the death knell of the couple'. But Maier's *No Kids* thesis goes beyond the standard moans about her life as a mother to issue more abstract cautions. 'You will inevitably be disappointed by your own child', she states. 'You can't stop yourself wanting complete happiness for your progeny. Children are dangerous. They will take you to court without a second thought' (Tucker 2007).

Maier's anti-natalism was greeted among UK commentators with the kind of bashful horror that follows the articulation of a self-consciously extreme position. Yet she was not seen as so extreme as to be unworthy of reportage—and many of her arguments chime with those being peddled in the name of worthy causes. Take her assertion that having children 'is also a vehicle for pollution and environmental destruction', involving cars, washing machines, and all the other 'gadgets' of modern parenthood. It is by no means rare today to hear the argument that the environmentally-conscious should avoid having children. In 2009, Jonathon Porritt, chair of the UK government's Sustainable Development Commission, made front-page headlines with his assertion that couples who have more than two children are being 'irresponsible' by creating an unbearable burden on the environment. Porritt, a father of two, said:

> I am unapologetic about asking people to connect up their own responsibility for their total environmental footprint and how they decide to procreate and how many children they think are appropriate (Templeton 2009).

In 2007, the Optimum Population Trust (OPT), of which Porritt is a patron, issued a report on this question (Templeton 2007). According to the OPT, if couples had two children instead of three they could cut their family's carbon dioxide output by the equivalent of 620 return flights a year between London and New York. This bizarre calculation reveals the connection between worthy environmentalism and the self-centred hedonism of many of Maier's other 40 reasons to remain childless. Having children is no longer something that we, as a society, take for granted that people will do and welcome the fact that they do it. Rather, procreation has come to be seen as a lifestyle choice, comparable to flying to New York or going to late-night dinner parties; and if people take themselves down this road, apparently they have only themselves to blame.

The Childfree v Breeders

The idea that children are just another lifestyle choice—and a dubious choice at that—reflects the gulf that has opened up between people who have children, and those who do not. Partly this is down to the fact that it is no longer expected that women will marry and have children early in their adult life, but that they will spend several years working full time and probably go back to work after maternity leave, leading to a clear generational difference in the workplace between 'normal' twenty-something women and the rather trickier thirty-somethings who have to leave the office at 5pm on the dot to get to their children's nursery, and are always off work battling chicken pox or some other childhood bug. Partly it is due to the fact that people are forming long-term partnerships later and women are having children later, which can mean that childlessness, in the words of the US writer Sylvia Ann Hewlett, can become a 'creeping non-choice' (Hewlett 2003). But these demographic changes, in and of themselves, do not explain the raft of resentment opening up between people who have children and those who do not—manifested in book titles like *The Baby Boon: How Family-Friendly America Cheats the Childless* (Burkett 2002), and complaints from young workers in Britain that they should have the same kind of 'work-life balance' rights in terms of being able to sleep off a hangover or go travelling for six months. Nor does it explain the out-and-proud identity of the 'Childfree': those who publish books like *Childfree and Loving It!* (Defago 2005) and *Baby Not on Board: A Celebration of Life without Kids* (Shawne 2005), or set up websites like Childfree.net, where they explain:

> We choose to call ourselves 'childfree' rather than 'childless', because we feel the term 'childless' implies that we're missing something we want—and we aren't. We consider ourselves childFREE—free of the loss of personal freedom, money, time and energy that having children requires (Childfree.net 2009).

The tension between the child-free and parents—often referred to, pejoratively, as 'breeders'—manifests itself in spats over working practices, state resources, and public space. Parents tend to react to this resentment either through cringing apologism or a bullish assertion of their moral authority, which is used by the childfree as evidence of why 'breeders' are unbearable.

This division is a result of the loss of a broader social vision about families and child-rearing, and a narrowing and one-sided appreciation of the idea of 'reproductive choice'. Reproductive choice has traditionally meant women's right to contraception and abortion—our ability to use medical technology to avoid being trapped into parenthood by a biological accident. Now, the notion of choice in relation to these matters is often interpreted to mean that anybody who has a child is supposed to have thought very carefully about it, planned out the timing and the practical and emotional consequences of their decision, and made all the appropriate adjustments to become the 'right' kind of parent. In this context, it is not surprising that parenthood is increasingly seen as an unattractive choice. Parenthood has come to be seen as such a daunting and oppressive task that anybody who doesn't feel able or inclined to subject themselves to such pressure finds it more acceptable than ever before simply to steer clear of the whole business. But the notion that children are 'chosen' with such deliberation means that parents are seen as making a lifestyle choice, and should just suffer the consequences in relation to the impact on their careers, social lives, and sleeping patterns.

The idea that families are a part of society, and that those who have children are making a welcome social contribution, is fading rapidly in favour of a much more individualised understanding that views parents and non-parents as opponents with conflicting interests. This is disturbing enough when it is a tension between those who have children and those who don't want/don't like children. More worrying, however, is the extent to which the stark division between parents and non-parents has come into play for adults who actively want to play a role in raising the next generation.

'Stranger danger'

Within a couple of weeks of my eldest daughter starting school at the age of four, I found myself confronted with a dilemma. She had invited one of her new friends home for tea: knowing nothing of this arrangement, this little girl's mother and I had an embarrassed conversation about whether we should organise this occasion for a future date, before deciding that I would just take the child home with me that night. As I was strapping the two girls into the car, it crossed my mind that I could be anybody. The mother didn't know me, where I lived, whether I had been cleared by the Criminal Records Bureau (CRB) of ever abusing children or whether I had a First Aid certificate in the event of accident or allergic reaction. When it was time for me to drop the child home I, like the other mother, was exhibiting visible signs of relief—not to mention no small sense of pride. We had crossed this hurdle; now we knew what to do.

Since then, of course, the business of play dates has become part of the unquestioned fabric of daily life. I routinely take random other children home with me, and my daughter is often picked up by a parent of one of these random other children after school and whisked across town, on the basis of informal arrangements made through scribbled notes in the children's schoolbags and hurried, harried conversations at the beginning and end of the school day. This taken-for-granted trust, based on the children's friendship with strangers rather than established relationships with people you already know, is for me one of the most exciting and rewarding aspects of my daughter's transformation from pre-schooler to school-girl. It was the point at which I recognised that being a parent is not something you do alone, with the only assistance from family, established and trusted friends, or according to paid arrangements with nursery nurses and babysitters. As parents, we are a group; for our children, a mass of adults whom they simply trust to look after them and facilitate their social lives.

But I cannot help wondering how long it will last. Already, it takes an effort of will to transcend the suspicion of other parents set in motion by schools. Remember the days when children ran out into the playground to be collected at the school gates? Nowadays, the rule operated by most primary schools in the UK is that children in Reception class must be released one by one into the arms of their parents, or whoever is the designated picker-up on that day. So before a play-date, you have to make sure to tell the teacher that your child will be going home with X, Y, or Z, and the teacher writes it down. When you huddle in the Reception playground watching the teacher nervously gripping each child by his or her shoulders until the designated responsible adult comes into view, you wonder what sense is transmitted to the children about who these adults might be, and what they might do to them. As for play-dates themselves — parents increasingly joke to each other that they have been 'CRB-checked' (vetted); it is only a matter of time before that declaration ceases to be a joke, and another parent's vetting status is routinely checked.

The widespread concern about what might happen if your child comes into contact with another adult is motivated by the panic about paedophiles who abuse children. To say this is a panic is not to be flippant. Home Office figures from 2002/3 — the figures still quoted on the NSPCC's website (NSPCC 2009) — show that 68 children were victims of child abduction by strangers, making up 9% of all child abduction offences recorded (Newiss and Fairbrother 2004). In 63% of these cases, the abducted child was recovered within 24 hours of being taken. The NSPCC notes that there are no available figures on the numbers of children who are abducted and killed by a stranger, because in such cases only one offence of homicide is recorded by the police. However, the charity acknowledges that 'the number of children abducted and murdered by strangers is almost certainly tiny':

> An NSPCC internal survey of newspaper reports of children who were killed or died in suspicious circumstances in the 12 months following Sarah Payne's killing (August 2000–July 2001) found that of 128 reported cases, not one was of a child abducted *and* killed by a stranger (NSPCC 2009).

The reason for the continued interest in child abduction statistics from 2002/3 may be because the total number of offences recorded by the police had increased by 45% on the previous year; and the main cause of this increase was in abductions attempted by strangers (accounting for 47% of the total). This could imply that more 'strangers' are out trying to grab children, and being foiled in their attempts to do so — or it could reflect changes in the way such crimes are recorded. This is certainly the view put forward by Newiss and Fairbrother (2004), in their analysis of the statistics published by the Home Office:

> The large increase in recorded stranger attempted child abductions may, at least in part, be attributable to the general move to a

more *prima facie* approach to the recording of crime (based on the victim's perception of a crime occurring). This has had an impact in several areas of crime recording, not least violent crime.

To put this another way: the increase in statistics of attempted child abduction may be a result of the police looking out for more cases of attempted abduction, and parents being more fearful of child abduction, and so thinking that they see strangers trying to abduct their children when they are not.

Of course, there have been some memorable, awful cases of actual child abduction: most recently, in 2007, the abduction of three-year-old Madeleine McCann from her bedroom in a Portuguese holiday apartment, and the abduction and murder of two schoolgirls from Soham, Cambridgeshire in 2002. The horror of these cases for the families concerned cannot be overestimated. But we all know that what the statistics say about the rarity of such events is true. We know this from the number of occasions our children are looked after by a wide range of adults without coming to harm. We know, simply by looking around us, that our world is not populated by predatory paedophiles, but by parents and other adults engaged in the daily business of protecting children, raising them and nurturing them. Yet the fear of the bad things that might happen to our children at the hands of people whom we don't know is wildly disproportionate to the comfort we gain from knowing the good things that actually do happen to children thanks to other adults.

Our overblown fear of the predatory paedophile is often described in the shorthand term 'stranger danger'. But the concept of 'stranger danger' has undergone a significant transformation in the past couple of decades. When I was a child in the 1980s, 'stranger danger' meant learning the mantra: Don't talk to strangers, don't accept sweets from strangers, don't ever get in a car with strangers, and if you get lost, ask for help from a lady or a policeman. This idea of the 'stranger' was never clearly defined, but we all knew what it meant: a lone figure, with no kids, who you really didn't know at all and of whom you, the child, should be suspicious. Nowadays, stranger danger is a concept that adults use in relation to filtering out potential dangers to their children, and 'stranger' means anybody you don't know really well. To put it another way: 'strangers' are everybody else.

Vetting and the institutionalisation of mistrust

The way that this new conceptualisation of the stranger has worked through parenting culture and policy in the UK is most clear in relation to the national vetting scheme — the requirement that all those working, or volunteering, with children undergo a check by the Criminal Records Bureau (CRB) to ensure that they have no record of child abuse. The CRB was established in 2002, initially designed to streamline the existing vetting procedures for teachers and other key professionals working with children. But over the subsequent seven years its remit expanded dramatically, to cover anybody who found themselves working with children in any capacity — whether as a paid professional, a volunteer, or merely somebody whose work brings them into contact with children. In November 2006, the requirement to vet anybody within breathing distance of a child who was not their own became statutory, as the Safeguarding Vulnerable Groups Act was passed into law. By 2009, the Independent Safeguarding Authority (ISA) had been established to run the nationwide process of mass vetting. And it really is mass vetting: as the literature published by the ISA clarifies, in order to avoid having to gain an official licence to work or volunteer with children, one would have to have no contact with children at all; and for an organisation to fail to carry out such checks is a criminal offence (ISA 2009).

The ISA vets all adults taking part in what has been termed a 'regulated activity', or a 'controlled activity'. Regulated activity means anything that involves 'contact with children or vulnerable adults frequently, intensively and/or overnight'. 'Frequent' means 'once a month or more', while 'intensive' means 'takes place on three or more days in a 30-day period'. 'Controlled activity' amounts to about the same thing, but applies not just to those working with children or vulnerable adults, but to those who happen to come into contact with them, for example:

> Frequent or intensive support work in general health settings, the NHS and further education. (Such work includes cleaners, caretakers, shop workers, catering staff, car park attendants and receptionists) (ISA 2007 and 2009).

How have we got to the point where it is assumed — and enshrined in law — that any adult coming into contact with children for more than a fleeting moment has to be given an official licence to do so, based on a formal check that he or she is not a convicted child abuser? Part of the answer lies in the politicisation of child protection measures by government ministers — as I show in the next chapter, the impetus for the national vetting scheme came from the shameless politicisation of the 2002 Soham murders, and the destructive impact of this policy is already being felt across communities. But while government ministers have a lot to answer for, they are not responsible for the speed at which the premise of mass vetting—that anybody you don't know should be suspected of having a nefarious purpose—has been accepted.

Touchy subject

In 2008, Frank Furedi and I conducted an investigation into the impact of the national vetting scheme and related child protection policy on community relations: specifically, the way that such policies shaped the ideas and concerns of those volunteering to work with children (Furedi and Bristow 2008). Those adults to whom we talked, involved in Guiding, youth football, church activities and many other forms of voluntary work, expressed a degree of frustration with the practical inconvenience of CRB-checking, and a scepticism about the ability of such technical systems to 'work', in the sense of being able to live up to the promise of preventing all potential abusers from having contact with children. Yet there was a general acceptance of the need for such a vetting scheme, articulated, in the words of one respondent, like this: 'It is sad but in this day and age it is necessary' (Furedi and Bristow 2008, p10). While these volunteers were clearly confident that they were not child abusers themselves, and that they had a lot to offer children—which was why they bothered to give up their time and energy—there was a palpable sense that it was simply responsible to regard everybody else, initially at least, as suspect. Where our respondents raised more discomfort was to do with the degree to which they themselves felt they were being regarded through the paedophile lens, as a result of child protection policies that advised them not to touch children, not to be alone with children, to be very careful in their interactions with children in case something became misconstrued. There was a sense that, even when the authorities take great pains to screen out anybody who is proven unsuitable to work with children, the level of trust placed in those who have passed this test is rapidly diminishing.

The extent of this discomfort has been documented by Heather Piper and Ian Stronach's astute critique of 'no touch' policies in educational institutions (Piper and Stronach 2008). Based on an ESRC-sponsored research project, *Don't Touch!* examines the extent to which those working with children are trained to view themselves through the paedophile lens from the outset. From the practice of wearing gloves to change a baby's nappy in a nursery to teachers in secondary schools taking care not to be alone with a pupil at any time, everyday interaction between children and their carers or teachers has become riddled with a sexual subtext. By training adults to view all physical contact with their young charges as something to be avoided, in case it becomes — or might be perceived as — inappropriate, adults are encouraged to apply a conscious check to every spontaneous interaction, as though it is only this formal check on their instinct that prevents them from crossing the supposedly thin line from child protector (teacher) to child abuser (paedophile).

Piper and Stronach are unapologetic in their assessment of the damage that the formalisation of previously taken-for-granted interactions between adults and children — a pat on the head, a cuddle, the application of sunscreen or a plaster — has on this relationship. The starting point for their investigation of this topic was:

> [T]he impression that the touching of children in professional settings had increasingly stopped being relaxed, or instinctive, or primarily concerned with responding to the needs of the child. It was becoming a self-conscious negative act, requiring a mind-body split for both children and adults, the latter being controlled more by fear than a commitment to caring (Piper and Stronach 2008, pviiii).

Their research not only confirms this impression of something wrong, but brings out the degree to which it is rapidly becoming normal behaviour for adults to hold back from children. Relations between (vetted, professionally-trained) adults and the children in their charge become governed, not by spontaneous actions of caring, but by self-consciousness and fear. Teachers do not trust parents or colleagues not to misinterpret a pat on the shoulder, they don't trust children not to make false allegations, and ultimately they cease to trust their own judgement of what is and is not 'appropriate'; so they hold back from touching children at all. This establishes a rule of estrangement, where adults charged with looking after children are encouraged, both tacitly and officially, to keep their distance and watch their backs.

Now consider how this process of estrangement plays itself out at a community level. As mass vetting becomes the norm, and with it the learned behaviour of holding back from children and looking over one's shoulder, the everyday interactions between adults and children become fraught with perceived danger. As anybody wanting to help out with their son's junior football team, accompany their children's class on an overnight school trip, or help to run a youth group becomes subject to a required process of training and vetting, those who fall outside the scope of regulated activity—for example, other parents organising play-dates—become the focus of suspicion and concern. The expansion of the vetting process to the community at large has already been put into action in embryonic form, under a pilot scheme in four districts of England where parents, carers and guardians have the right to ask the police whether somebody who has access to their children has ever been convicted for sex offences (Casciani 2008). As was widely reported, this 'somebody' can mean everybody from a babysitter to a boyfriend, introducing the mind-boggling scenario of single mothers finding themselves under pressure to run a CRB-check on their partner.

Unfortunately, whether vetted or not, adults have already picked up on the need for excessive caution in interacting with other people's children—a situation that reached its horrific conclusion in 2006, when two-year-old Abigail Rae was found drowned in a garden pond, having wandered off from her nursery. A bricklayer had driven past her as she wandered, and thought about whether he should go back to help her; he decided not to because 'I thought someone would see me and think I was an abductor' (*Daily Mirror* 2006). The Abigail Rae story has already entered folklore as an example of the dangerous consequences of child protection policies that, by estranging generations and encouraging responsibility aversion on the part of adults, put children more at risk of becoming lost, injured, upset, even killed. Yet despite this grim reminder of why adults need to trust themselves and each other to look out for children, the dynamic that drives both policy and parenting culture is one that seeks to separate adults from children even more.

Chapter Seven

Parenting Policy

Case studies in mistrust

From the popularity of *Supernanny* to the bitchiness of the Mommy Wars, many of the trends that I have discussed in this book have their roots in a cultural malaise, which stokes up division and suspicion between parents and encourages us constantly to question our own abilities and motivations. To view government policy as the simple cause of this malaise, and to imagine that a different policy approach would make things suddenly all right, would be wrong. However, the rapid developments in parenting policy and child protection policy are not merely reflections of a negative cultural turn. These developments enjoy what therapists would like to call a codependent relationship with modern parenting culture, in the sense that policymakers feed off the prevailing anxieties about raising children to create policy that deepens these anxieties and exacerbates the problems.

One of the remarkable aspects of parenting policy is the sheer amount of it. For example, the Department for Children, Schools and Families lists 28 new publications published in December 2008 alone (DCSF 2009: Accessed 31 January); and to examine parenting policy in its entirety is beyond the scope of this book. But a brief examination of three major policy initiatives, introduced within the past decade, is enough to reveal the degree of misanthropy and mistrust that underwrites policy that purports to 'support families', or 'protect children'. Two are sweeping national policies that came into force in Britain under the broad remit of child protection. Both were sparked by rare, horrendous cases of child abuse and murder. Between them, these policies provide for unprecedented levels of scrutiny and regulation of relationships within the family, between children and their primary carers, and relationships outside of the family, between children and those who work or volunteer with children. Together, they add up to an official view that no adult can automatically be trusted to take care of children: the relationship is presumed to be abusive, until it can be proven otherwise. The third noteworthy policy is the flagship of New Labour's therapeutic state: the Sure Start initiative, which endeavours to deal with the problems caused by poverty and social disadvantage by helping people to become 'better parents'. What all three policies have in common is the extent to which they have politicised parenting, marshalling horror stories and prejudices to justify interventions that have no hope of achieving their stated goals, but which will intensify the assumption that unregulated interaction between adults and children is deeply problematic.

Parents as villains: Every Child Matters

The *Every Child Matters* policy framework, published as a government Green Paper in 2003, is a thorough-going review and reorganisation of services and monitoring procedures of all children and young people in Great Britain. Every area of life accessed by children and young people, from education to health to social services to leisure activities, is now governed by the principles of *Every Child Matters*, which are officially summarised as follows:

- Be healthy
- Stay safe
- Enjoy and achieve
- Make a positive contribution
- Achieve economic well-being (ECM 2009a).

A core plank of *Every Child Matters* is 'information-sharing' between state agencies, in order to 'protect children and young people from harm and help them achieve what they want in life'. One outcome of this is the creation of a gigantic central database, ContactPoint, on which information about all children will be stored.

The presentation of *Every Child Matters* is fluffy, benign, and generally appears rather nice. Of course every child matters; and why shouldn't children's services try harder to be more coherent and effective? But a look at the history of this policy framework, and the way it works in practice, presents a rather different picture.

Every Child Matters was the policy outcome of a major government inquiry, by Lord Laming in January 2003, into the murder of eight-year-old Victoria Climbié by her carers (Laming 2003; ECM 2009b).

The murder of this little girl in February 2000 shocked the nation—and rightly so. Victoria was brought to England in 1999 by her aunt, Marie-Therese Kouao, to 'get a better life' (Laming 2003, para 1.1). Victoria suffered a horrific catalogue of abuse at the hands of Kouao and her boyfriend, Carl Manning, finally ending up in the intensive care unit at St Mary's hospital in Paddington, where she died with 128 separate injuries to her body. In January 2001, Kouao and Manning were convicted of murder and child cruelty, and sentenced to life imprisonment.

The Laming Inquiry into the circumstances that led to this child's death pulled no punches. The first page of the report details the scale of abuse that Victoria suffered, including a quote from Dr Lesley Alsford, the consultant responsible for Victoria's care on the occasion that she died, who said, 'It is the worst case of child abuse and neglect that I have ever seen' (Laming 2003, para 1.5). When it came to the question of who was to blame for this, Laming was similarly uncompromising. While acknowledging that professionals engaged in child protection work are doing a difficult job, made more so by the fact that child abusers will often go to great lengths to hide the impact of the abuse, he argued that 'Victoria's case was altogether different': Victoria was not 'hidden away', but her injuries known to a number of agencies and professionals, all of whom could and should have intervened earlier in the situation (para 1.16). Laming noted:

> In his opening statement to the Inquiry, Neil Garnham QC listed no fewer than 12 key occasions when the relevant services had the opportunity to successfully intervene in the life of Victoria. As evidence to the Inquiry unfolded, several other opportunities emerged. Not one of these required great skill or would have made heavy demands on time to take some form of action (Para 1.17).

During the Inquiry, news reports detailed an appalling record of incompetence, cowardice and evasion on the part of those individuals and agencies that had both the power and the remit to protect children against abuse—including a police officer who worked for Haringey Child Protection Team and was responsible for Victoria's protection, but refused to visit her home because she was worried she might catch scabies (an unpleasant, but easily treated, skin disease) (BBC News Online 2001). The clear finding of Lord Laming's report was that Victoria Climbié's death represented 'a gross failure of the system' of child protection (Laming 2003, para 1.18). The authorities had more than enough information about Victoria to give them cause to intervene, and more than enough power to do so. Yet they did, effectively, nothing to protect this little girl.

If there are any positive aspects of this grim case, these are that cases such as Victoria Climbié's are incredibly rare—which is what makes them so shocking—and that the child protection systems already in place provided ample opportunity for the authorities to prevent the abuse going so far. One might have expected, given Lord Laming's findings, that the agencies and individuals named as having failed Victoria would have been brought to account. What actually happened was that the British government shamelessly exploited Victoria's case to bring about a thorough reorganisation of children's services, in a move that affects every child and every service and has absolutely nothing to do with dealing with rare, severe cases of child abuse. Rather, it presumes that every child is a potential victim of child abuse, and demands official monitoring and intervention from the cradle to the grave.

Take, for example, the proposal for the ContactPoint database: a project that has cost a reported £224 million to date (Bennett and Frean 2009). This initiative has been promoted as a direct outcome of the *Every Child Matters* proposal for greater 'information sharing' about children, the idea being that if the various agencies involved in Victoria Climbié's case had pooled the information they had about this child, problems would have been identified and dealt with earlier. Many people have voiced objections to ContactPoint—with very good reason. Dr Eileen Munro, reader in social policy at the London School of Economics and an expert on child protection, has from the first been highly critical of the attempt to link the government's overhaul of child protection services to the Victoria Climbié case. 'Would Victoria Climbié have been saved if the changes proposed in the children's green paper had been in place? The sad answer is no', wrote Munro in 2003, before going on to argue that rather than asking hard questions about the deterioration of child protection services, the *Every Child Matters* framework proposes overhauling the 'superstructure' of children's services: with unhelpful consequences for professionals and children alike (Munro 2003). In the Climbié case, frontline staff had plenty of information about this little girl's injuries and concerns about their causes—the problem was that by their own admission, staff did not bother to read the documents. But while 'information sharing' would not have saved Victoria, and there is no evidence it will prevent similar rare cases from happening again, the national database has the potential to cause huge problems for millions of other children and their families.

The drive to record every concern about every child will lead to information overload, where professionals are under pressure to flag up every concern that they might have about every child 'just to be on the safe side'. This will inevitably lead to families being suspected of abuse where there is none, and creating so much work for professionals that they are blinded from those cases that really do require intervention (Munro 2003). There are also major privacy concerns: not least because of the government's well-documented track record of losing sensitive data. When it was revealed in January 2009 that 400,000 people would be given access to the ContactPoint database, parents, security experts and opposition parties voiced alarm. 'Creating more bureaucracy with sensitive information accessible to hundreds of thousands of people will do nothing to improve child protection', argued Michael Gove, the Shadow Education Secretary, while David Laws, the Liberal Democrat children's spokesman, said bluntly: 'This intrusive and expensive project needs to be scrapped' (Bennett and Frean 2009).

Beyond the children's database, many other aspects of the *Every Child Matters* framework are proving controversial, and it can by no means be assumed that this policy helps children more than it harms them. In broader policy areas, the *Every Child Matters* framework is being expanded to provide blueprints on every aspect of a child's care and development—no longer, it seems, with the modest aim of preventing child abuse, but with the aim of creating the optimal child. In 2007, the government launched the statutory 'Early Years Foundation Stage' (EYFS). The EYFS, widely described as a 'toddlers' curriculum', sets 69 goals and more than 500 development milestones that children should reach between birth and the age of five (Woolcock 2008; EYFS 2009a). While it pays lip-service to the fact that children develop in slightly different ways from each other, in practice the document indicates exactly what children should be doing during any one phase, and exactly what the 'practitioner' should be doing to make that happen (DfES 2007; EYFS 2009b).

In November 2007, a group of academics joined forces to complain about the proscriptive nature of the Early Years Foundation Stage, arguing that it had been introduced 'by stealth' and that its over-emphasis on formal learning at an early age would harm children's development rather than enhance it (Woolcock 2008). Certainly, the document seems to have been introduced with wilful disregard to the long-running debate about the value of Early Years education, which indicates that hot-housing children to read at the age of three cannot be assumed to create geniuses later in life. But the problems that this statutory framework seems likely to cause for teachers and other parenting practitioners pale into insignificance compared to its impact upon parents.

The EYFS is aimed at all registered early years providers and schools, who have been required to use it from September 2008. But it is a document that lays out what is considered to be the optimal process of child development and adult interaction over the whole period of birth to the age of five—a period in which, historically, most children have been at home with their parents, outside of the remit of formal education and care. With the government's insistence on the importance of parenting classes and bringing children into a more formal childcare setting from at least the age of three, it is clear that the traditional home-with-mummy phase of a child's life is going to become less and less of the norm. And when children are home-with-mummy, mummy will be expected to behave more like a professional carer or 'practitioner', with her eye firmly trained on meeting her child's developmental goals. Increasingly, parenting will be both farmed out to professionals, and parents themselves will be professionalised.

Somehow, a policy that was inspired by 'the worst case of child abuse and neglect ... ever seen', and an inquiry that exposed the manifest failings of state agencies to act upon clear signs of that abuse, has become a policy that seeks to help parents help their children find their tummies and force early years workers to follow a centralised play-plan. *Every Child Matters* will not stop rare cases of horrific abuse: as evidenced by the tragedy of Baby P in 2008, who, like Victoria Climbié, was a resident of Haringey Council and within the sights of child protection workers, yet died following an appalling catalogue of abuse. But *Every Child Matters* has already made all those living or working with suspicion the targets of surveillance and intervention, to ensure that they are doing their utmost to create the government's identikit child.

Dangerous Strangers: The national vetting scheme

On 17 December 2003, Ian Huntley, a former school caretaker in the Cambridgeshire village of Soham, was convicted of murdering 10-year-olds Jessica Chapman and Holly Wells. The girls' murder, in the summer of 2002, became a national horror story; and as the sub-

sequent trial unfolded, the errors, incompetence and obstructive PR
stunts evident in the police investigation horified us again. Following Huntley's conviction, it became clear that this was a man with a
dubious past, who had come to the attention of the authorities on
several occasions: he had been accused of having sex with four
underage girls, of raping four women and indecently assaulting an
11-year-old girl. Sir Michael Bichard was mandated to 'urgently
enquire into child protection procedures in Humberside Police and
Cambridgeshire Constabulary', in particular 'to assess the effective-
ness of the relevant intelligence-based record keeping, the vetting
practices in those forces since 1995 and information sharing with
other agencies' (Bichard 2004, para 3).

Bichard returned six months later with a raft of recommendations
that revolved around one key proposal: that to limit the likelihood of
another Soham, those people intending to work anywhere near children should be treated like criminals from the start. To this end, the
report recommended setting up a national police intelligence system
to share information between forces about suspect individuals — in
Huntley's case, those whom the police may have suspected of committing an offence, but who were never convicted. The report also
called for a social services database to log all those suspected of
abuse, for a government register of those wishing to work with children, and for a further tightening of the already-stringent vetting
procedures. Bichard even floated the idea of a 'card or licence' to be
issued to individuals working with children — though he conceded
that 'it is not for me to decide on this issue', he suggested that should
such a licence be issued, 'a card with a photograph and biometric
details would provide real advantages in checking identity'
(Bichard 2004, para 4.124).

It is of course possible to look back in horror at what we know now
about Ian Huntley, and wonder at the stupidity of a system that lets
somebody like him work in a school. But as Ross Clark pointed out in
The Times (London) at the time of the Bichard report:

> [T]here was a good reason why Mr Westwood and his staff did not
> go about telling all and sundry that Huntley was a vicious sex
> offender. Until the conclusion of the Soham trial in December,
> Huntley had never been convicted of any sex offence (Clark 2004).

Huntley had been suspected and accused of several crimes, but 'in a
free society, the weight of allegations does not equal guilt'. Clark's
point is a crucial one, going to the heart of our criminal justice system. Yet disturbingly few even seemed aware of this, let alone both-

ered by it. A round-up of reactions to the Bichard Report, published by the *Guardian*, brought together quotes from the children's minister, the Liberal Democrat home affairs spokesman and the president of the Association of Chief Police Officers, all of whom fulsomely welcomed the proposals and, if anything, criticised the government for not introducing them sooner (*Guardian* 2004). Only Dr Mary Bousted, general secretary of the Association of Teachers and Lecturers, raised a concern about ever-more stringent checks on those working with children—but she quickly brushed that aside. 'It would be a pity if vetting procedures put off volunteers who can have so much to offer schools, but this may be a price that has to be paid', she said.

It does not take a detective to work out that the sweeping measures proposed by Bichard would not necessarily stop another Huntley from committing his horrendous crime. As the string of sex offence accusations indicates, Huntley had no great difficulty in getting access to younger girls before he became a school caretaker; and for all Bichard's emphasis on closer monitoring of those who work with children, he is forced to cite the fact that Huntley 'had *not* previously held any post involving significant contact with children' as grounds for suspicion [my italics] (Bichard 2004, para 31). The report's introduction recognises that, for all the focus on institutional cock-up and systems reform, an individual determined to kill will do so:

> Huntley alone was responsible for, and stands convicted of, these most awful murders. None of the actions or failures of any of the witnesses who gave evidence to the inquiry, or the institutions they represented, led to the deaths of the girls (Bichard 2004, para 5).

The reason Sir Michael Bichard's proposals have been so widely endorsed has very little to do with Ian Huntley, or the rare horror of the Soham case. Rather, it is because Bichard's contention, that 'one cannot be confident that it was Huntley alone who "slipped through the net"' (Bichard 2004, para 6), has been accepted across the board. This assumption, that Britain is full of hidden Ian Huntleys—or, to put it another way, that there is a bit of Huntley in us all—creates a climate in which everybody is to be seen as a potential paedophile or child-killer. And with the Safeguarding Vulnerable Groups Act 2006, the assumption that anybody who wants to work with children must have their motivations scrutinised has become national law. The consequence of this, as I argued in the previous chapter, has been the rapid institutionalisation of mistrust of all adults — to the point where people who have the noblest motivations regarding children find themselves discouraged from volunteering to help with extra-curricular activities, comforting a child who is upset, or helping a child in danger.

Parents as victims: Sure Start

When New Labour came to power in 1997, one of its flagship phrases was 'social exclusion'; and the flagship policy designed to deal with this problem was Sure Start. By 1998, a massive £524 million had been allocated to spend on the programme over three years (Belsky, Barnes and Melhuish 2007, p11); between 1999 and 2004, £1907 million was allocated to 524 programmes in the most disadvantaged communities in England (Schneider, Avis and Leighton 2007, p9). To complete the spending spree, a team at Birkbeck University, London, was awarded £20 million and rising to evaluate the scheme as it went along (Ward 2005).

But what was Sure Start? Just as New Labour's concept of 'social exclusion' was from the outset amorphous and slippery, so Sure Start as an intervention designed to tackle social exclusion was impossible to define. The basic premise of social exclusion was that the most significant problem facing families in circumstances of economic deprivation was not their lack of money or employment, but the negative behaviour that they manifested as a result of being disconnected from the agencies of the state. Policies designed to tackle 'social exclusion' therefore sought ways to reach the 'hard to reach' through therapeutic mechanisms such as education or advice-giving. By a similar token, the aim of Sure Start was to ameliorate the consequences of child poverty by encouraging better parenting and forging relationships between families in the most disadvantaged communities and the state.

In 2005, the Birkbeck team released its first evaluation of the programme, beginning an interesting lesson in government-inspired evidence-based policy. The evaluators found that Sure Start had not delivered on any of its major goals: it failed to boost pre-schoolers' development, language and behaviour, and it actually had an 'adverse impact' on 'children from relatively more socially deprived families (teenage mothers, lone parents, workless households)' (Belsky *et al* 2006). Discussing their findings in a journal article, Belsky *et al* wrote:

Socially deprived families with greater personal resources may have been better able to take advantage of SSLP [Sure Start Local Programme] services and resources, which may have left those with fewer personal resources (such as young mothers and lone parents) with less access to services than would otherwise have been the case. Relatively more socially deprived parents may also find the extra attention of service providers in SSLP areas stressful and intrusive (Belsky *et al* 2006).

Further, the authors noted that, while '[m]ore children and families were affected beneficially than adversely' by Sure Start, as teenage mothers, lone parent families and those living in workless households 'formed a minority of the sample', this was slim grounds for comfort:

[B]ecause the most socially deprived groups account disproportionately for many problems in society (such as school problems and crime), the apparent adverse effects of SSLPs might have greater consequences for society than the beneficial effects (Belsky *et al* 2006).

Right-leaning critics of the scheme, such as Melanie Phillips and Minette Marrin, had a field day with these findings, claiming that this was evidence that the government is tearing apart the family for no discernible benefit. But the government perspective rallied, with a spirited piece by *Guardian* columnist Polly Toynbee. Toynbee focused on the one positive finding from this study — that Sure Start mothers demonstrated a degree of 'warmer parenting' than the control group (families in deprived areas where Sure Start schemes did not yet operate), exhibiting 'less hostility, less smacking, less negative criticism and more affection' (Toynbee 2005). She then defended the scheme on the grounds that a) the evaluation did not compare children actually in Sure Start programmes, only those living in the area, many of whom had no contact with it; b) the US Head Start scheme for deprived youngsters, which inspired Sure Start, showed no improvement until the kids reached adolescence; c) the fact that Sure Start mothers demonstrated 'warmer parenting' 'may prove vital in the long-run'; and d) these things are really difficult to evaluate anyway. Toynbee concluded that Sure Start's lack of demonstrable success so far only indicates how important the programme is, and the need for greater government investment.

Toynbee's commentary was a classic example of having it both ways. More than that, though, her convoluted arguments proved how novel an intervention Sure Start actually was. For when it comes to Sure Start, what counts is not the outcome but the process.

Sure Start's aim is not to transform the fortunes of poor children: how could it, when the one solution to child poverty — giving parents more money — is conspicuously absent in its approach? Its aim is gradually to transform the relationship between the family and the state. In this sense, the evaluation of Sure Start is as important as the scheme. By focusing on such questions as parenting style as an outcome measure, the Sure Start evaluation makes explicit that the goal of such a policy is not to eradicate poverty, provide childcare, or any such tangible things. It is all about putting parenting style — 'warmer parenting' versus 'negative parenting' — at the heart of the policy agenda; popularising the idea of parental causality as the only way of keeping children in work and out of jail.

As the National Evaluation of Sure Start (NESS) continues, it seems that the Birkbeck team might be finding other 'positive' outcomes. At a seminar given in January 2009, Jay Belsky, Research Director of NESS, described how parents in Sure Start areas have a greater 'utilisation of support services'. In other words, the 'hard to reach' are maybe now being reached: and that, in the terms of this particular brand of therapeutic policy-making, is a key marker of success.

Of the three policy interventions discussed above, Sure Start is, in my view, the most insidious and damaging. While people kick — however weakly — against the prescriptions and excesses of *Every Child Matters* and the national vetting scheme, there is little opposition to Sure Start outside of a vague cynicism about whether it will 'work' as a solution to poverty. Clearly, it will not. Even if those parents who have improved their 'utilisation of support services' have become nicer/warmer/less 'negative' parents as a result, it requires a narrow and fanciful view of the world to think that this means that children born in poverty will have dramatically improved life chances. Even if we could assume that money counts for nothing, so many other factors impact upon children as they are growing up that the effect of pre-schoolers having a couple more books in the home, or a bit less shouting, is negligible. All this amounts to the government passing the buck for dealing with social inequality, by blaming the parenting practices of those in deprived areas.

Beyond that, the calculated process at work in the Sure Start programme of gradually wearing down parents' independence of official advice and support, and re-making their relationships with their families in accordance with the dominant parenting orthodoxy, speaks to the disdain with which policymakers see the private relations of family life. Sure Start carries a high financial cost—even back in 2005, the scheme was reportedly worth £3 billion (Ward 2005)—and it is heartbreaking that the money being poured into shiny new Children's Centres with strings attached could so easily be spent on the childcare infrastructure Britain so badly needs. But even that financial cost is nothing compared to the way the scheme has legitimised an idea no classic right-wing government ever dreamt of being able to pull off: making social inequality the fault of individual parents, and using their poverty as a means to rule their personal lives.

Chapter Eight

Standing up to Supernanny

Even people in high-flying jobs go on management training, they go on training courses. It doesn't mean to say they are bad at their jobs; it means they are worth training because the company believes in them. And if parenting is going to be the future of this country I think it's a job very worth training for. *Sarah Verney, the Hampton Trust, discussing the launch of the National Academy of Parenting Practitioners* (Littlemore 2007).

I always say to people that the job of Prime Minister is difficult, and sometimes I think the job of Home Secretary is worse … but the job of being a parent is difficult, whoever you are and whatever your situation. *Then UK prime minister Tony Blair in Watford, delivering a landmark speech on 'improving parenting'* (Blair 2005).

The combination of intensive parenting culture and policy that continually seeks to professionalise and scrutinise parenting practice has led to the widespread idea that parenting is a 'job', requiring a particular skill-set and a clearly-defined level of contractual obligation. The idea that parents need training is explicitly discussed in relation to parenting classes—and was made official with the government's National Academy for Parenting Practitioners, launched in November 2007. As children's minister Beverley Hughes put it:

Parents can learn a lot from each other about their children, and parenting programmes make for fascinating television, but for real help that makes a difference, parents need support from someone who is properly trained. That is why the new national academy is going to play such an important role (NAPP 2007).

But parenting is not a job, and to present it as such represents a fundamental misunderstanding about the nature of family life. Professionalising parenting in this way demotes parents from authorities on their lives and those of their families to mere 'partners' in child-rearing with officials who presume to know best. This idea of parents as partners of the state is wrong—both morally and empirically. There is a real difference between the parent-child relationship, which is intimate, emotional, unconditional and profoundly human, and the relationship between a professional, practitioner or teacher and a child with whom they are employed to work.

How do we challenge the professionalisation of parenting, and reclaim childrearing as a relationship based on spontaneous affection and authority? How do we break out of the prison of the Kindergarchy to reclaim the role of family as a 'haven in a heartless world'? There are no easy answers, and no quick policy fixes. But there are some obvious places to start.

The need for privacy

Back in 1977, the American sociologist Christopher Lasch criticised those who assumed that the family's 'isolation' from the public sphere makes it 'impervious to outside influences'. 'In reality, the modern world intrudes at every point and obliterates its privacy', he wrote:

> The sanctity of the home is a sham in a world dominated by giant corporations and by the apparatus of mass promotion. ... Increasingly the same forces that have impoverished work and civic life invade the private realm and its last stranglehold, the family (Lasch 1977, pxxiii).

Lasch understood that the dynamic between society and the family, and the basic contradiction this contained, meant that even 30 years ago it was impossible truly to see the family as a separate, private sphere untouched by market forces. However, the understanding that a certain amount of privacy and autonomy were necessary for family life to play its desired role was not a sham in the most fundamental sense: the clear demarcation that this implied between the family and the state. Even while the domestic sphere was besieged by advertising and the ethos of consumption, the ruling elite retained a clear sense that the state meddled at its peril.

How that has changed. From the Sure Start initiative, designed to insinuate itself into family life in order to facilitate 'better parenting', to the idea that parents are mere partners with the state in the project of child-rearing, the privacy of family life these days is presented as the very problem that needs tackling. The idea seems to be that if only families were transparent, like the ones we watch on *Supernanny*, there would be less scope for bad parenting practice and more openness to experts telling us how to do things 'right'.

But if the cult of *Supernanny* and clones tells us anything, it is that families who open their doors to the world lose the ability to behave normally. What we see on TV is not real, but edited highlights of incompetence and redemption; how we behave when under scrutiny is not spontaneous or authentic, but an act put on to please the viewers. The intensity of family life, with its everyday ups and downs, is such that it cannot withstand being conducted as an act. We need space to be ourselves, in order to create a space in which children can develop themselves. In short, we need to get *Supernanny* out of the living room and Sure Start out the front door, and to reclaim our family lives as a space for living rather than acting.

The need for trust

Families need privacy, but they also need each other. One of the most bitter ironies of recent policy developments is the way that the refrain 'families are increasingly isolated' is offered as an excuse for intervention by the authorities, while policy actively works to increase families' isolation from each other. Raising children is not supposed to be the sole responsibility of individual parents inside four walls—it is a generational responsibility, which requires that we help other adults and expect that they will help us in turn.

The problem of 'trust' is often discussed in relation to government agencies, state bodies, and other professionals. But people are right to be wary of vast government databases or midwives proffering diagnoses of Post-Natal Depression—and if anything we are rather too trusting in this regard. Where the lack of trust is a real problem for parents is in our diminishing capacity to trust each other. From paedophile panics to the assumption that every one of our child's needs should be met in a particular way by a particular person at a particular time, we have become increasingly unwilling to allow other people to have a relationship with our children. This narrows our children's experience of life and increases the burden of pressure on parents.

Increasing trust between adults requires initiatives both at a policy level, and at the level of how we, as parents, think and behave. The policy implications are straightforward. The raft of new, highly politicised and deeply pernicious initiatives that work to destroy spontaneous trust relations between adults should be abolished, and the millions of pounds spent on these initiatives should be diverted into the establishment of a flexible, affordable childcare infrastructure that would enable mothers and fathers to work as much as they want or need to, while encouraging the idea that other adults can be trusted with the care of children in the early years. A government with the right vision could create a wonderful childcare network out of the funds freed up simply by the abolition of the Independent Safeguarding Authority, the ContactPoint Database, and the Sure Start project — all it requires is the political will to make that happen.

For parents, building trust with other adults requires a reality check, and a leap of faith. It means recognising that the vast majority of adults do not pose a threat to our children, and taking account of the positive role that other adults can play in expanding children's experiences and reducing some of the practical burdens on ourselves. It means helping other children when they are hurt or frightened, and telling other children off when they are causing trouble. It means organising play-dates, engaging in voluntary work, and rejecting the impulse to reach out to professionals as the first line of support. It means, above all, trusting ourselves to do right by our own children, without endlessly seeking guidance and reassurance from the growing army of Supernannies on our doorsteps.

Towards a grown-up discussion

The assumption at the heart of policy-making and much media commentary is that most families are, to all intents and purposes, dysfunctional: parents lack the right attitude, they can't cope, they need advice and monitoring in relation to every little thing they do with their children. Family policy has become family therapy, while the practical issues to do with time and money are effectively ignored. Parents have become infantilised; and their role is seen as less to raise their children than to act as on-the-ground mediators of official advice.

But while parenting culture treats us like children, we do not behave like children — and that is the silver lining in this dark cloud. There is a basic contradiction between the task of raising children — where you have to behave like an adult — and a culture that keeps telling you that you don't know what you are doing and you should be seeking support. This is why parents get into such a state of guilt and unconfidence, but also why standing up for ourselves takes less than one might imagine. We can insist on acting like adults in the face of so much cultural belittling, and rejecting the idea that other people — parents, non-parents, sexual partners, children — are the problem. We are still family — and we have more in common with other families than anything that divides us.

PART TWO

Reflections on the Parenting Debate

Tracey Jensen

Why do People Watch Supernanny?

Why are people watching programmes such as *Supernanny*? To answer this, one might put that very question to a representative group of people, as an Ipsos MORI poll, conducted on behalf of the National Family and Parenting Institute, did in 2006 (NFPI 2006). This report found that huge numbers of the population were tuning in to parenting television shows, 'with *Supernanny* emerging as a clear winner', watched by 42% of all adults.

Many people reported that they were putting into practice the parenting techniques suggested by these programmes, that the programmes served as reassuring comparisons to their own family lives and that they welcomed the suggestions made; although the survey also found that 'sizeable minorities' of respondents expressed their uncertainties about the advice, or concern for the welfare of the children that participated in such programming. The report concluded that those producing and commissioning such programmes have a responsibility towards an entire generation of adults, suggesting perhaps a return to the ethics of public service broadcasting, with an emphasis on education.

In my work I attempt to explore in more depth the relationships between the parental identities formed during the experience of viewing such programmes and the networks of meanings that are circulated through the content and technologies of the programmes themselves. I interviewed parents about their experiences of and relationship with contemporary parenting advice—specifically the genre of parenting television—and I then watched an episode of *Supernanny* with them. My intention has been to map in more complex ways how parents relate to parenting television and its tenets, and the kinds of identity statements that are occasioned by these narratives.

The Ipsos MORI survey — though in some ways a useful tool — presumes that the viewing population can have a rational, cognitive and clean response to *Supernanny* and its peers, and that researchers can quantify these responses with a set of questions. Having watched *Supernanny* with many parents, I would argue that our encounters with these programmes are anything but rational and cognitive. The visions of failure that circulate through and within these programmes beckon to the viewer in visually immediate ways and invite reactions that are bodily, emotional and affective.

The parents who participated in my research laughed and gasped with the horror of recognition; moaned, groaned and sighed in sympathy with the spectacle of weeping parents; and tutted and shook their heads in disbelief at the conduct of the families on the television screen. Moreover, the emotionally rich texture of these viewing encounters complicated — and often contradicted — the diplomatic and considered narratives of their own parenting that they offered during the interviews before. By employing the interview *and* textual encounter method in tandem, we are able to complicate our tidy conclusions about why people are watching.

Parenting television programmes present parenting as a formulaic set of skills that can be learned within a fixed time-frame and according to a set of universally applicable principles. From one episode to the next, parenting becomes visually confirmed as a way of erasing socio-economic differences and guaranteeing that once all children are 'parented' according to the same principles, the experience of *all* families is better, happier and more productive. These notions are embedded within the contemporary cultural moment that we live in; a therapeutic moment which demands that we become deft in the management of our hearts, articulate in emotional vocabularies and confident, competent governors of our psychological health (Rose 1999).

Government ministers have interpreted the popularity of these programmes as evidence that parents want support in learning the 'right' ways to interact with their children, without attending to the great deal of identity work that is done through these visual encounters. This identity work includes judgement, pleasure, investment and reassurance, but it cannot be reduced or known through interview alone. The Ipsos MORI survey upholds the notion that parenting television can be understood as a democratic popularising of parenting advice that would previously have been delivered through pamphlets, books and manuals; and that, as such, programme-makers have a responsibility to educate appropriately.

I would argue that the very visuality of these programmes sets them apart from other kinds of advice (though they are, of course, a legacy of the industry) in complex ways. They represent a specific moment in therapeutic culture in which 'parenting' has taken centre stage as a mechanism through which the interior psychological health of our families may be ruminated upon, and the psychological health of families on the television screen may be held out to judgement and scrutiny. The complex and uneven ways in which the parents from my research viewed, assessed and articulated themselves in conversation with the ideas of these programmes suggests that the visual encounter with parenting television — much like encounters with instructional, how-to-live, reality television more generally — constitutes another site in which difference is lived.

The parents with whom I worked certainly brought their complex histories, biographies and investments to the programme, but they also did a great deal of identity work *through* their encounters with the programmes. Responding to the narrative drama on the screen became an opportunity to situate oneself within the contemporary parenting landscape. In a sense, expressing preferences or distrust of particular parenting techniques serves as a metaphor for other kinds of social difference.

Nodding in agreement, or otherwise, at the Naughty Step technique for example (which *Supernanny* has helped to popularise, and which indeed has become a cultural shorthand for the programme) enables parents to position themselves in relation to discourses around child development, lifestyle, gender and social class. For some parents, the disciplinary focus of *Supernanny* became a theme of their criticism of the programme, whilst for others it provided a comforting notion that the complexities of everyday life can be remedied and rendered knowable through a set of simple rules, a how-to guide or a recipe for living.

Being able to articulate their specific parenting philosophies through engaging with the programme, and referring to other televisual examples with which they were familiar or preferred, was an instance of the display and deployment of specific cultural competences and capitals. The dynamism, fluidity and emotional texture of these uneven television encounters, and the conditions under which parents were able, or not, to 'stand up to Supernanny', means that it is more important than ever to attempt to produce a 'sociology of television' (Morley 1992) and not simply a semantic account.

References

Morley, D. (1992) *Television, Audiences and Cultural Studies*, London: Routledge.

NFPI (National Family and Parenting Institute) (2006: October) The Power of Parenting TV Programmes—help or hazard for today's families? http://www.familyandparenting.org/page/item/document/8/1.

NFPI (National Family and Parenting Institute) (2006: 15 October) 'Exclusive poll for NFPI shows influence of TV parenting programmes'. http://www.familyandparenting.org/item/1284.

Rose, N. (1999) *Governing the Soul: shaping of the private self* (2nd Edition) Free Association Press.

Jennifer Howze

How 'Good' Parenting is Hurting Children

Poor parenting is a bit like obscenity — we all know it when we see it. Witness the gym-slip mother smoking a fag while dandling her toddler; the father smacking his young son for misbehaviour; the couple who sit and sip their tea while their children run riot through the café.

On the far end of the scale there are terrible parents who abuse, neglect and fail to nurture their children — necessitating that as a society we intervene. Yet for the vast majority of parents the issue of poor parenting is much more nuanced.

'Bad' parents are naturally, by definition, not good parents. But 'good' these days has actually come to mean 'perfect'. It means forever thinking of your children's welfare, feeding them according to the latest nutritional standard, always responding to tantrums with loving tact and serene patience, endlessly stimulating them with appropriate activities, the list goes on. These are undoubtedly good goals for parents. The problem is that mothers and fathers must affirm their status as 'good' parents by making the 'correct' decision in every interaction with their child. Good parenting has become a state that needs to be continually renewed, moment to moment with every decision, with 100% success.

That means that in any given day there are a thousand opportunities to backslide into being a bad parent. Scream at your child to put his shoes on? Give your two-month-old baby formula? Let your daughter watch a few hours of TV? Establishment experts condemn these actions and news stories appear practically every week advising that they damage children in some way.

Ignore the experts at your peril. We've become more dependent on their advice for childrearing — dished out in books, television shows, magazines articles and even advertisements — so that we've come to define success as a parent as literally doing it by the book, whether the volume in question is written by Gina Ford or Dr. Spock.

We have turned parenting into a series of tasks and decisions that must be done 'right' if we are to fulfil our role as 'proper' parents. It doesn't just begin in the child's infancy. These days it starts at birth — did you have a natural birth, cut the cord and bond immediately with the baby on your chest? And even earlier. Knock back a glass a wine during pregnancy and you're choosing your own selfish desires over the wellbeing of your child — despite the fact that even the experts can't even agree on how moderate drinking affects unborn babies.

This thinking creates a climate of uncertainty and fear. Parents start to feel they cannot make a decision unless it is backed up by a theory in the latest parenting bestseller. Every decision becomes fraught. They worry that packing crisps in the lunch box might encourage a dependence on salty, fatty foods and result in a lifetime of obesity. (This is despite the fact that they ate crisps themselves growing up and somehow survived.)

Additionally, this thinking reduces childrearing into something of a recipe. All the messy, unwieldy, occasionally painful and some-times magical parts of bringing up a child are being homogenized into a rulebook that makes it more like baking a cake or creating a spreadsheet. Plug in the right ingredients or digits, the thinking goes, and you'll get the perfect outcome.

And in some ways it alienates us from our children. Avid readers of parenting advice manuals would be forgiven for thinking that the under-18s are a peculiar genus to be studied, experimented on (with behavioural corrections) and manipulated, rather than small, not very experienced humans who need advice from the tall people in their household. Why shouldn't children occasionally see mum and dad lose their temper? Why shouldn't the routine slip once in a while? That's what happens in the real world.

It's time we encourage parenting that turns out children who can contribute to our society and play well with others — whatever their age. We should encourage ourselves and others to take risks and fol-low different paths when necessary — no more looking down our noses at those who do it differently.

Of course this also means accepting, within reason, things we don't like. We must accept that to some extent parents have the right to raise brats and jerks. But if the freedom to follow our hearts means we're more confident, better (that's not to say perfect) parents, then we and our kids will be that much more adept at living in the real world, warts and all.

Christina Hardyment

Parenting 'Experts'

Where they came from and why we need them

The important thing to understand about the so-called 'experts' who deal with parenting is that most of them are self-appointed. It is essential to enquire where they come from: in the same way you need to ask of any research reported in newspapers: 'How many people were involved, or was it just the boy next door?'.

The history of parenting advice goes way back: in fact some of my favourite books are from the seventeenth century and written in rhyming couplets. So what has changed about parenting advice today? What I learnt from my study of two hundred years of child-rearing advice in Britain and America is that such advice has always been related to the prevailing social, technological, economic and moral climate. Most was in written form, although today's health visitors are direct descendants of the philanthropically-inclined upper- and-middle class women who toured their less fortunate neighbours with baskets of fruit, soap, disinfectants, medicaments and improving Christian tracts, and who organised schools for them. They were not always welcome, but in the days before social services they did a great deal of good.

We have enjoyed in Britain some 50 years of unparalleled economic prosperity. This is the age of the individual: religion has, if you believe the media, gone out of the window, although it still powerfully shapes childrearing practice in some of our Communities. But childcare manuals now rarely have chapters dealing with moral matters. We're children of the universe, with a right to be happy. We're educated to fulfil ourselves, and have brilliant careers. To make this more possible, all our eggs now tend to be in one or two baskets: families have grown far smaller, because of effective contraception methods. We have higher expectations of domestic comfort and satisfying personal relationships. We are also a mobile society, moving away from parents and friends whenever a new job or attractive house beckons.

This trend towards individualism has made this the age of the expert. We now feel we need 'professionals' to tell us what to eat, what to wear, what to read, where to go on holiday, how to find the right partner, and of course, how to bring up babies. Especially that, and for very good reason. Few new parents have had close encounters of an intimate kind with babies; nor do babies fit easily into the enjoyable individualistic way of life they have been living. There is slick talk of maternity leave, career breaks made to sound as easy as coffee breaks, and childcare provision. But once you have your own baby in your arms, things tend to fall apart. Personally I feel that new parents face an impossibly unrealistic script: high debt levels often force them to compromise their parenting ideals.

An additional difficulty is the sheer volume of advice. The latest research on parenting hits the headlines of newspapers, is broadcast on the radio and television, flashes up on the internet. There is a huge amount of it, and it is constantly changing like an aggressively-edited Wikipedia article. The good news is that you can always find advice that suits what you instinctively feel like doing, if you look hard enough. Don't be fooled into thinking that one size fits all.

But what happens if we've lost confidence in those instincts? Roll on Big Brother—not the let-it-all-hang-out TV reality show, but an Orwellian rain of directives from on high. The greatest of all experts is no longer God, but the Government. We deplore the idea of the nanny state, but we seem to demand to be nannied in every aspect of our lives, and none more than when it comes to parenting. Such demands come from the best of motives. We are aware that not everything in the garden is rosy. With historically unique generosity of spirit, we want everyone to be well-off, well-behaved, happy. We don't like hearing about feral teenagers on sink estates, or drug-addicted 11-year-olds in rural backwaters. We want everything to be perfect, so we rely on experts to tell us how to do it—and flagellate ourselves when we fail.

I think we should go on trying to improve things, but emphasis the positive rather than the negative. Things haven't got worse. There has not been a dramatic increase in child murders and abductions, it's just that they now makes national rather than local news. Children are better educated than they have ever been. Most parents do a great job in difficult times, and are dreaming up new kinds of networks, like online friendships, to create their support systems. We need to boost their confidence, not deplore their shortcomings.

Nancy McDermott

The Tyranny of 'Parenting Science'

If you look at any discussion about parenting in the USA right now, one idea is so all-pervasive that most parents don't notice it or, if they do, they think it is a good thing. This is the 'tyranny of science' — the blurring of the line between science and morality, so that people have started to look at science for providing a universal standard, whereas they might previously have looked at institutions that are more traditionally associated with those things: the church, the state, and the family itself. The result is that The Science, which appears to exude a rational and objective standpoint, has become the reference point for virtually all the experts on childrearing in the United States.

In one sense, science and childrearing have been linked for some time. From the moment when the eugenics movement first launched campaigns to 'grow better babies' to JB Watson's experiments in conditioning 'little Albert' and today's focus on neuroscience and brain development, science has gone hand in glove with each succes- sive wave of childrearing orthodoxy. But unlike in the past, when it was primarily parenting experts or the authorities looking to science to bolster the case for their particular agendas, today The Science has become essential for parents themselves.

Unfortunately, when one looks at The Science of parenting debates, it becomes clear that what appears to be scientific is any- thing but. This trend has contributed to creating an unstable and destructive culture of parenting that affects the way that parents relate to their kids, the way that they relate to one another, and the way that they relate to the rest of society.

A case in point involves the reaction to an article published in the science section of the *New York Times* in October 2008, which reported on a new study in *The Archives of Pediatrics and Adolescent*

Medicine. The study suggested that running a fan in the room with a baby reduces the risk of Sudden Infant Death Syndrome (SIDS) — also known as 'cot death' — by 72 per cent. The study, as the article itself pointed out, doesn't really add anything to our understanding of this rare and tragic phenomenon. If you control the sleep environment — things like whether the baby sleeps on its back or with a comforter — the presence of a fan in the baby's room is statistically insignificant. But that didn't stop it from becoming a huge point of discussion for parents across the USA.

Among parents in my own neighbourhood, we discussed the rate of SIDS internationally, the merits versus the risks of co-sleeping, the difference between cause and correlation and the meaning of statistical strength. We might have been an expert panel — except we weren't. We were just parents; parents who spent their evenings Googling the rate of SIDS and the prevalence of co-sleeping in different parts of the world; parents weighing 'the evidence' and, ultimately, parents seeking to justify our own decisions about where and how and with whom our children slept. This exchange was particularly 'sciencey', but like any discussion about parenting, it had an emotional intensity a world away from actual scientific discourse.

It is pretty apparent that we are not talking about SIDS any more. We're talking about validating or defending the personal preferences of the parents in this discussion. And I think it's a measure both of how unconfident parents feel and how much science is now revered that even a random study about SIDS can call into question individual parents' choices about how they put their babies to sleep.

The impact of parents' reliance on The Science for clues about how to behave has been significant. While many people instinctively recoil from preachy moralism, adding science to the mix has confused matters. Parents consequently feel obliged to treat the pronouncements of researchers and parenting 'experts' with far more seriousness than they deserve. The proliferation of these moralising theories sporting a 'scientific' gloss has led to a groundswell of scepticism. Blogs like Mainstream Parenting Resources and Rational Moms have sprung up to offer a refreshingly critical take on the so-called 'science of parenting'.

However, challenging bad science alone is not enough. The problem is not bad science *per se*, but the way that parents' relationship with science is steeped in moral significance. They cannot take it for granted nor can they escape its tyranny in their daily lives. It may be that the most 'rational' course of action for parents in these circumstances is to rely first and foremost on their own judgement and leave contesting science to the scientists. That may at least help to make bringing up children seem less fiendishly complicated.

Zoe Williams

Parenthood as a Career?

This is one of those untestable theses that journalists love to expound,
but it strikes me that parenting today has become overheated. People
take their roles as parents so seriously that the role has accrued this
quasi-professional status — professional because it suddenly requires
expertise, training, workshops, government guidance; quasi because
it's still unpaid, it's still personal, it's still intimate. Because it would be
trite to wonder why people love their children, we tend not to ask,
why do people take their children so incredibly seriously? But this
question is worth asking, or at the very least: when and why and how
did we develop this pressing orthodoxy, this sense that there must be
a single path of righteousness, a Way Things Are Done, which any
right-thinking person would follow, and would follow as the abiding
principle of their identity. Perhaps I'm being nostalgic, but it strikes
me that, when I was a child, the business of raising children was
viewed as one element under the umbrella of living one's life: it was
something that everybody did differently and, moreover, people rev-
elled in their difference. One's individualism was a cornerstone of
one's identity; people didn't strive to follow a true path, less still did
they hinge their moral character on doing it right.

Elizabeth Gilbert wrote, in an otherwise awful book, *Eat, Pray,
Love*, that since feminism tore up the rule book, there's been no
template for women's behaviour anymore. There is no template for
when you should be working, when you should be home with
children, when you should be in a relationship and so on, so every
woman's choices are taken as an indictment of every other woman's
choices: we think we are going about our business, but in fact we are
accusing each other with our behaviour.

I think this is true, and it becomes marked in the area of parenting.
There is no such thing as a choice that might fit one parent and might
not fit another parent, and mothers especially are incredibly vocal
about one another. Even decisions as similar as a childminder or a nursery — you see incredibly vicious, bitter arguments both in the media

and between individuals about these choices. I certainly do not think that there should be a parenting rule book. But because that ground is in flux, is being continually contested, we have nothing to judge ourselves on apart from other people's shortcomings, which we consequently have to spend a lot of energy itemising, often extremely harshly. The struggle to shore up one's own worth by continual downward comparisons becomes a quest for orthodoxy — how do you know they're doing it wrong, basically, if you don't believe in a 'right answer'. In trying to create a gold standard, you open the door to seeing yourself as not just the mother or father of the child, but the perfect mother or father of the child, the template mother or father of the child.

If you look at this question in the broadest possible brush strokes, in the olden days it was considered that intelligent women didn't look after their own children — someone did it who was, well, not more stupid, necessarily… let's just say, better adapted to messing about, poster paints, repetitive pursuits. Now, there's a desire to reclaim the business of childrearing as something that both rich and intelligent women might want to do, and most of us would applaud this: you miss a lot if you eschew spending time with your children. And a lot of the activities that displaced it weren't so headily intellectual anyway, they were just playing bridge and spinning more money. But there is a residue of shame in childrearing, a defensive and understandable drive to deny that it's menial, to wring meaning from it. And in order to justify that, parents seem to bring a level of brisk, critical, professional engagement which the task simply doesn't require. I realise this is a controversial statement, more controversial than my tone really allows, and I realise that there are credible, respectable voices arguing that there is no task more intellectually stimulating than childrearing, but I simply don't agree. It's stimulating, all right, but it's not intellectual. The MMR scandal is a really good example of over-engaged people taking things too seriously, micro-managing decisions that are not theirs. Mothers 20 years ago didn't look at the medical profession with this kind of scepticism, as a malign, careless body. I don't want to say 'doctor knows best', but ultimately, yes, research does know best. That's why people do it. Once your identity rests on your perfection as a mother, on your uniqueness, then suddenly there's this burden of proof. How do you demonstrate that you're perfect, unique? By delegating nothing, by deferring to no one, by unleashing the full force of your critical judgement on a task that you will personally undertake to inflate until it warrants your scrutiny. And that's how you end up with a child with measles.

I think the ageing population has had a major impact. In the UK in 2005, the fertility rate of women in their thirties outstripped that of women in their twenties, for the first time. This makes a difference because people take themselves more seriously the older they are — no I do not have figures on that, but it's true anyway. I simply know. Furthermore, in your twenties you would not completely obliterate yourself for your child. You would not think, 'All my efforts are going to go into this child'; you would still think of yourself as a person in the middle of a life. The current model, for middle-class women at least, is more phasic and less pell mell. People think 'I'm going to get everything done, I'm going to achieve all my career hurdles, I'm going to do all my travelling, all my partying, and then I'm going to have children' — it has created this atmosphere where you set the self-gratification of your early life against the self-abnegation of your child-bearing years. It's amazing to me how often you will read parenting commentary expressing sentiment to the effect of 'why did you have them, if you didn't want to look after them?'. To say 'I want to look after them sometimes, but other times I want to do something else' is the most horrific statement, now, whereas I think a generation ago that would have been, firstly, a reasonable statement, and secondly, in the context of an active women's movement, trammelling into the workplace, an important statement.

As a culture, it seems that the discussion about children becomes more sentimental and overheated the less we talk about politics. Everyone has this drive where they are altruistic in some situations and self-interested in others, and when we had a superstructure of the Left, people could talk about putting themselves second to society. The Right could make a case, also, for their ground having been eroded — the conservative concepts of civic duty and community. From both sides, then, these outlets for selflessness have been rather abruptly shut off, and where we need an element of martyrdom for our own self-building, we focus it entirely on our children. It has become acceptable, natural, to talk about 'wanting the best for your children'. I think a generation ago that would have been a ridiculous thing to say because it's just like saying, 'I want the best for me'. It has become meaningful to talk about how much you love your children and how you'd do anything for them, because that's the only area in which your selflessness can be expressed. Quite aside from the way this has tainted the way we approach bringing up children, it often seems to have poisoned the relationship between parents and the childless. But that's a debate for another time.

Helene Guldberg

'Cotton-wool Kids'

Who started it?

Parents today are criticised for not giving their children the right kind of love and attention and for not sufficiently protecting them from a never-ending list of risks. And now they are criticised for over-anxiously keeping their children tied to their apron strings.

One of the claims in the Children's Society's *Good Childhood Inquiry* is that children are becoming hostages to parental fears (Children's Society 2009). In 2008, an ICM survey commissioned by Play England reportedly showed that over-cautious parents are 'spoiling' children's playtime (Play England 2008).

It is undoubtedly the case that children and young people today are given less and less freedom to roam outdoors with their peers. There are far fewer kids out and about on street corners or in parks unaccompanied by adults. Research by Colin Pooley at Lancaster University shows that the area in which children are allowed to play has shrunk over the years (Pooley 2006). In the 1940s children were allowed to roam freely over a far wider expanse. Today children are more strictly controlled by their parents: few of the young children interviewed by the researchers had dealt with many risks, and compared with earlier generations they had not had the opportunity to learn to negotiate or to deal with challenges.

There is a real danger that by cocooning, over-protecting and over-supervising children, society might be denying the next generation the opportunity to mature and develop into capable, confident adults. I feel strongly that children are losing out on many childhood experiences that my generation took for granted. But I also feel that in pinning the blame on individual parents and their 'over-cautious' anxieties those who decry the decline of outdoor play are being unfair — and naive.

The cause of the 'cotton-wool kids' phenomenon is a broader cultural obsession with risk, which has had a major impact upon policymakers, public institutions and media debate, as well as upon teachers and parents. And in challenging this culture, it is important to be clear about where the real problem lies, and to resist pat explanations for its cause.

Parental fears must be understood in the context of a generalised sense of anxiety and risk-aversion, which is particularly strong when it comes to the lives and futures of children. One worrying outcome of this culture of fear is that children could grow up to fear the outside world. Indeed, the Lancaster University researchers found that today's primary school-age children voice a number of concerns about playing outside unsupervised — in particular about being abducted or run over. What a contrast with respondents who had been the same age in the 1940s, who recalled how they 'swam in dirty canals and played in air raid shelters and did not tell their parents about encounters with "flashers"' (Pooley 2006).

A survey of 800 children aged between four and sixteen carried out by the Children's Society and the Children's Play Council in 2001 found that 25 per cent were put off playing outside for fear of being bullied by older children, and 17 per cent felt unable to play outdoors because of the dangers of traffic (BBC News Online 2001). And *A Child's Place*, a report by the think-tank Demos and the Green Alliance, found that children are keen to spend more time out of the house but are often too frightened to do so — associating being outdoors with danger (Thomas and Thompson 2004).

Ironically, if children miss out on opportunities for developing a sense of risk and danger, and taking more and more responsibility for their own lives, they are likely to be at even greater risk when they eventually are let out in the 'big bad world' without having learnt essential skills. The US writer Hara Estroff Marano, editor-at-large of *Psychology Today*, highlights the danger of making life easier for children in the short term: all you end up doing is making it harder for them in the long term (Marano 2005, p4).

By putting too much onus on keeping them safe, adult society could be denying children the opportunity to grow up and face life's many challenges. Children and young people do need to be given gradually more freedom and responsibility so that they have the opportunities to show what they can do on their own. It is not just the outside world that is presented as dangerous and risky. For example, because of the growing obsession with bullying children are pushed to look upon their everyday encounters with their peers—friends or enemies—through the prism of potential violence and abuse.

Through unsupervised play children are given the opportunity to acquire skills such as co-operation and competition that are mainly learned through interactions with equals. Unless children are given the opportunity to engage with each other without adults hovering over them they won't really learn the consequences of being clumsy, nasty or thoughtless, or how to cope with good-natured teasing or spiteful and hurtful behaviour. We do children no favours by protecting them from all those experiences that may be distressing, or even risky, and that come with everyday life. But we would do them a real favour by expecting more of them and gently easing them into living life to the full—even if it entails getting some emotional or physical bruises along the way.

References

BBC News Online. (2001: 2 August) 'Fears "keep children indoors"'.

The Children's Society (2009) *The Good Childhood Inquiry*. http://www.childrenssociety.org.uk/all_about_us/how_we_do_it/the_good_child hood_inquiry/1818.html.

Marano, H. E. (2004: November-December). 'A nation of wimps'. *Psychology Today*.

Play England. (2008: 4 August) 'New figures for Playday 2008 reveal children deprived of adventurous play'. http://www.playengland.org.uk/Page.asp?originx_7663lg_88857648193x4s_200883188v.

Pooley, C. (2006) *A Mobile Century? Changes in Everyday Mobility in Britain in the Twentieth Century*. Aldershot: Ashgate Publishing.

Thomas, G., and Thompson, G. (2004) *A Child's Place*. London: Demos/Green Alliance.

Val Gillies

Is 'Poor Parenting' a Class Issue?

Questions about class and 'fitness to parent' illustrate a peculiarly contemporary twist to the age-old tradition of blaming the poor for their plight. Judgements around good and bad parenting have quite insidiously ingrained their way into our culture so that now childrearing is commonly viewed an objectively learnt skill that you either pass or fail in. The government has enthusiastically embraced this idea, training up a whole new workforce of professionals to promote what they refer to as 'parenting best practice'. Leaving aside the soulless aim of translating intimate family relationships into a technical exercise, this approach wilfully ignores the value-laden nature of parenting.

In short, my understanding of good parenting might not match yours, and herein lies the real issue. Parenting values and experiences are heavily influenced by class. The 'parenting best practice' literature reflects the world view of its middle-class creators. In fact the very idea that you can grade parenting outcomes (i.e. a child) is indicative of a very particular value system held by the middle class elite that populates the government. From their perspective, the badly parented inherit cultural and personal defects that confine them to poverty and crime. Hence tackling social problems is as simple as providing parenting classes. Following this staggering over-simplistic logic working-class parenting is condemned as poor because their children are less successful in life. There is absolutely no evidence to support this.

Of course the other side of this coin is the belief that the success and privilege of the middle classes stems from their competent upbringing and personal strength. This is not just a comforting idea. It drives the moral crusade that lies behind the current politics of parenting. Parents (we are talking mothers in the main) who do not conform to middle-class ideals are viewed as letting their children down. A distinctly contemptuous and punitive tone characterises much of the policy rhetoric around parenting. This has prompted and fuelled derision and disrespect towards working class mothers. They are often the butt of cruel humour, portrayed as promiscuous, irresponsible, indifferent to their children's needs and just plain dumb.

My research with marginalised mothers reveals a very different picture. Mothering is testing in any circumstances, but managing with very little money in poor housing in deprived areas generates problems and challenges few privileged parents properly conceive of. Raising children in these circumstances requires commitment, considerable self-sacrifice and resilience. It also demands a flexibility and resourcefulness that perversely leads to accusations of bad parenting. As a result we see mothers berated for — amongst other things — harsh discipline strategies, a lack of involvement with children's school work or a determination to feed them unhealthy food.

These are issues I have written about in some length before, but I will attempt to summarise my arguments briefly here. Middle-class democratic parenting approaches tend to be counter-productive for working-class families. The emphasis on choice makes little sense where there is none, and the focus on equipping children with reasoning and negotiation skills is often risky. It can encourage children to challenge adults. Defiant middle-class children might be seen as precocious or naturally struggling towards independence, but their working-class counterparts (particularly boys) might well find themselves locked up as a serious threat to society.

In terms of education, working-class mothers tend to stay away from schools for very good reasons. They feel they have little to contribute and quite reasonably think teachers should be responsible for their children's education. But more importantly, why should they be expected to invest in their child's academic performance when the odds are so stacked against success? We have an education system that depends of some children failing. Success is a relational concept dependent on the failure or ordinariness of others. Working-class children tend to fail so their middle-class counterparts can succeed.

This is particularly the case now that the advantages middle class children enjoy have been legitimised and justified morally through an expectation of parental involvement in education. A middle-class focus on education makes sense as an effective way of passing privilege down through the generations. Such parents access considerable resources to cultivate their child's academic performance. In contrast, working-class children are educationally disadvantaged from the beginning. There is little their parents can do about this other than help them deal with failure. Unlike the middle classes they can not draw on their own knowledge and experience, garner respect and attention from teachers, access support from their social networks, move house for a better school or pay for tutors or special needs assessments.

Appeals for disadvantaged parents to become more involved in their children's schoolwork ignore this fundamental inequity, with moral aspersions cast on those who opt out of a game overwhelmingly loaded against them.

This issue around diet is often illustrated by images of the mother who sabotaged Jamie Oliver's healthy school dinners campaign, by pushing pies and chips through the railing. This was generally met by the middle classes with horror and incomprehension. But is it really so hard to understand the emotional significance of food, especially to mothers? Many parents (including myself) were brought up on what is now viewed as a dangerously unhealthy diet. These mothers and their children are likely to associate this food with love, pleasure, warmth, safety and all the other comforts of family life. For working-class pupils, the foods condemned as unhealthy offer an important link with home, and this allows mothers to feel reassured that their children are being properly cared for. This is clearly a cultural as well as a financial issue. Chips, pies, burgers and sausages have long made up the staple diet of British working class families.

This brings me back to the issue of values. The politics of parenting is not just an attempt to regulate family life. It is also a concerted effort to eradicate lifestyles and choices that the government views as distasteful and backward. It seems that poverty and disadvantage is tolerable but the poor themselves are not.

Jan Macvarish

The New Parenting Orthodoxies

Class and social mobility have become a kind of alchemy in recent years. In the absence of any actual political demands being made, the needs of the poor, the working class or 'the excluded', as they have come to be known, have become the subject of economists' and social scientists' formulae. Social mobility has come to be discussed as a kind of snakes and ladders game: going to museums, breast-feeding, having Harry Potter on the bookshelf, and eating carrots push your offspring up the social ladder; going to the shopping centre, using formula milk, watching television, eating pizza are snakes down which your offspring slide. Inequality has become a mystical code to be unlocked from the outside by complex analysis of 'risk factors' and 'social capital'. Explanations which focus on unequal access to material resources are cast as being crude and out-of-date, whereas newly identified factors, such as emotional resilience, social networks and above all, parenting, have become key to discussions of social mobility and in particular, 'child poverty'. The reduction of social inequality to 'child poverty' is interesting in itself; abstracting children from their families while simultaneously blaming 'poor parenting' for the perpetuation of 'child poverty'.

The way in which the poor are referred to in policy discourse as the 'socially excluded', the 'hard to reach' or as 'vulnerable groups' reinforces the idea that these people possess deficient moral or psychological characteristics and are also passively unable to help themselves. In the wider culture, we can see the poor increasingly portrayed as a passive lump who drag the rest of us down with their fat, emotionally illiterate, McDonalds-eating, bullying children. It often appears that policy-makers think that Vicky Pollard (comedy series Little Britain's 'chav' teenager) actually exists: Health Minister Beverly Hughes claimed to have heard stories of young mothers smoking to reduce the birth weight of their babies while Hazel Blears talks of 'Shameless' families, with reference to the Channel 4 comedy about a poor, dysfunctional Manchester family.

Critics of social policy rightly claim that holding up 'middle-class' lifestyles as the ideal way to insure against poverty is a gross reversal of causation. The logic of current policy thinking is that if people who are poor are so because of their 'poor' lifestyles, it must be the case that the better off are so because of their 'better' lifestyles. Therefore, policy 'encourages' the poor to adopt the alleged traits of the socially successful, such as singing nursery rhymes to babies, reading to children, cooking from scratch and engaging in 'open communication' with teenagers.

While the critics are right to point out that this flips causation on its head, and blames the poor for their poverty, they are also wrong on two counts. First, this critique implicitly accepts the notion that the middle-class parents are culturally distinct from the working class and somehow have a monopoly on nurturing relationships with their children. In this world-view, the middle classes offer a uniquely intimate and positive culture of child-rearing, and are particularly adept at simple life-skills such as cooking. Prejudices about the working class being socially 'broken'; alienated from familial support and the intergenerational transmission of functional family behaviour, and incapable of socialising their children are reinforced. But second, it also denigrates legitimate aspirations for educational achievement as 'middle-class pushiness' and flattens out the humanising and enriching cultural capital that the middle classes tend to be better able to access.

It could be argued that the most notable feature of the current obsession with 'parenting' is that the dividing lines are not clearly drawn along class lines, but between those who comply with the new orthodoxies and those who can't or won't. There is something in the characterisation of 'problem parenting' for most people to look down on — whether that is letting kids play out on the streets or allowing them too much 'screen-time' within the home, leaving them home alone or 'helicoptering' them, returning to work 'too quickly' after birth in order to pursue one's own career or living out our thwarted ambitions through our children.

When I interviewed teenage mothers, surely one of the most stigmatised groups of parents today, they were able to elevate themselves to a moral high ground by contrasting their youthful energy and commitment to mothering in contrast to those 'older' mums who were too tired to play with their children or who dumped their children in nurseries all day. While these mothers clearly had a stake in doing down other mums as inadequate in a zero sum game of parenting ability, there is a mirror-image of this counter-stigmatisation in competing claims for 'vulnerability': for example, the focus on teenage pregnancy was challenged recently on the basis that the youngest mums may be very well supported; those who really struggle, it was argued, are those in their early twenties. Similarly, older mothers are sometimes said to experience more problems because they are more isolated, anxious and have higher expectations of motherhood. Bringing up teenagers is often claimed to be more demanding than the toddler stage of parenting by those arguing for greater parental rights to leave in the workplace. Thus the category of the 'problem parent' is ever-expanding.

Of course, the intolerant culture of politicised parenting will hit those at the bottom the hardest; those who have most contact with the state. But it impacts on all parents (and non-parents or future parents) and is extremely divisive. It relies on the imagined deficiencies of 'other parents' — who don't read with their children, who put only a Snickers bar and a can of Coke in the lunch box, who shout 'too much' or even smack. Moral parables of parental inadequacy are readily available in the media, in the blogosphere and at the school-gate to fuel our imaginations. The new orthodoxies are likely to be embraced most vigorously by those who express their aspirations by consuming the markers of enlightened parenthood and this is not confined to the middle classes. The appetite for having our own parenting affirmed as 'good' ensures that the politics which holds up the 'bad' for castigation while reflecting our anxieties about what 'successful' parenting means resonate more than ever before.

Ellie Lee

The Normalisation of Parent Training

Where I work at the University of Kent I co-ordinate a research project called Parenting Culture Studies. The aim of this project is to establish *parenting culture* — that is, the social norms and mores surrounding child-rearing — as an object of study in its own right.

Over the past few years the discussion I have had most often is about what, if anything, is distinct about parenting culture today. In my view today's parenting culture is different to the past. What is peculiar to this point in history is that bringing up children is seen as being far too difficult and important to be left to parents. A dominant view is that a third party needs to be involved. This is a far more powerful social view than it used to be. When I make this observation, a lot of the time people respond by saying, 'Yes ... but no. There have always been experts telling parents what to do and parents have always felt very worried about what they are doing. So it's not that new'.

It is of course true that there have always been child-rearing experts, and Christina Hardyment's book *Dream Babies* provides the best account of the history of this. But there is something very distinct about this aspect of parenting culture as it has developed over the past 15–20 years. First there are a lot *more* experts. Second, from the perspective of developments in social policy, there's also something else that becomes rapidly apparent. The presumption of social policy is that *parent training* is needed by all. The idea informing policy is that being trained can and should be a normal part of parental experience. As a result, we have the emergence of a new army of parenting professionals.

In the UK there is now a National Academy of Parenting Practitioners — a new place where parenting professionals can go to learn how to train parents, funded by the government. One of its main areas of work, according a press release about it, is 'training, development and support for a parenting workforce' — this is made up of 'parenting practitioners' and, rather bizarrely to my mind, those who, we are told, 'train the trainers'.

To my knowledge we have never had a parenting workforce before. Beyond this, there is a redefinition of the job of a range of professionals to include parent training as part of what they do. This is very important for health professionals. The role of nurses and midwives has changed a lot over the last decade, becoming much more overtly about training parents from the point of conception, even pre-conception, about their responsibilities and the ways they should behave. In education also, schools have been charged with the role of shaping parents' attitudes and behaviour, as well as teaching children. This is a very notable development.

Some have criticised some aspects of new interventions to train parents, on the grounds that they are stigmatising or that they have a 'one size fits all' approach. For example, parenting classes have been criticised from that point of view. However, these criticisms are far too weak, because they assume that parent training is fundamentally a necessary enterprise; it is just how you do it that is at issue. Hardly anyone is taking up the rationale for, and the effects of, what seems to me to be a fundamental change in the *modus operandi* of social policy. There are four key areas which, in my view, should be subject to more interrogation and debate.

The first is the claim that the reason why we need parent training is because the family has changed beyond all recognition in the past 20–30 years. Yet the change in the family over recent history is not all that great when compared to other historical epochs, where the family has been much more challenged and fragmented than now. Furthermore, while trends such as people having children later in life are important, it is by no means clear why they should automatically lead to the need for parents to be trained in child-rearing. Changes in family size, marriage rates, age of childbirth and so on are now simply assumed to mean parents are less well equipped to raise children that in the past. There is no reason to assume this.

The second area worthy of interrogation is the claim that 'the evidence' tells us we need parent training. This rests on the idea that there is such a thing as a science of parenting to which we can look — often discussed in relation to brain science — which proves we need all of this parent training. This claim ignores the contested nature of much of the science in this field, and seeks to prevent discussion through presenting policy interventions as based on incontestable scientific fact.

The idea that parenting is the source of all social problems is, third, a critical area for debate. Government policy documents now routinely claim that 'poor parenting' is more important than anything else in causing a range of social problems. This is a new sort of determinism unparalleled in its over-simplification, and it is striking that politicians can get away with placing the cause of social problems at the doors of individuals' parenting styles without more people criticising this idea.

Finally, the most important area to critique is that parents are a risk to their children, because knowingly or unknowingly they do things that fall outside of the established orthodoxy. Sometimes this refers to practical things that parents do, such as feeding their children the 'wrong' things or drinking alcohol when they are pregnant. What is most worrying to me, however, is the idea that our emotional engagement with our children is of the wrong sort. There is more and more discussion now in policy documents that we feel the wrong kind of way about our children and that we need a therapeutic education to get us to feel in the right way. The fact that parenting policy has become about regulating emotion as well as behaviour indicates how truly insidious this trend is.

References for Part One

Books

Arney, William Ray. (1982) *Power and the Profession of Obstetrics*. Chicago and London: The University of Chicago Press.

Belsky, Jay, Barnes, Jacqueline, and Melhuish, Edward. (2007) *The National Evaluation of Sure Start: Does area-based early intervention work?* Bristol: The Policy Press.

Bennetts, Leslie. (2007) *The Feminine Mistake: Are we giving up too much?* New York: Hyperion.

Blair, Cherie. (2008) *Speaking for Myself: The Autobiography*. London: Little, Brown.

Bowlby, John. (1988) *A Secure Base: Clinical applications of attachment theory*. London and New York: Routledge.

Burkett, Elinor. (2002) The Baby Boon: How Family-Friendly America Cheats the Childless. Free Press.

Calman, Stephanie. (2005) *Confessions of a Bad Mother*. London : Macmillan, 2005.

Campos, Paul F. *The Obesity Myth: Why America's obsession with weight is hazardous to your health*. New York: Gotham Books.

Collier, Richard and Sheldon, Sally. (2008) *Fragmenting Fatherhood: A socio-legal study*. Oxford and Portland, Oregon: Hart Publishing.

Cusk, Rachel. (2001) *A Life's Work: On Becoming a Mother*. London: Fourth Estate.

Defago, Nicki. (2005) *Childfree and Loving It!* Vision.

Douglas, Susan J and Michaels, Meredith W. (2004) *The Mommy Myth: The idealization of motherhood and how it has undermined* women. New York: Free Press.

Eyer, Diane E. (1992) *Mother-Infant Bonding: A Scientific Fiction*. New Haven and London: Yale University Press.

Figes, Kate. (2000) *Life After Birth*. London: Penguin.

Freely, Maureen. (2000) *The Parent Trap: Children, families and the new morality*. London: Virago.

Friedan, Betty. (1963) *The Feminine Mystique*. London: Victor Gollancz.

Fitzpatrick, Michael. (2004) *MMR and Autism: What Parents Need to Know*. London: Routledge.

Furedi, Frank. (2001) *Paranoid Parenting: Why ignoring the experts may be best for your child*. London: Allen Lane.

Furedi, F and Bristow, J. (2008) *Licensed to Hug: How child protection policies are poisoning the relationship between the generations and damaging the voluntary sector*. London: Civitas.

Gard, Michael and Wright, Jan. (2005) *The Obesity Epidemic: Science, Morality and Ideology*. London and New York: Routledge.

Green, Jane. (2001) *Babyville*. London: Michael Joseph Ltd.

Green, Jane. (2004) *The Other Woman*. London: Michael Joseph Ltd.

Green, Jane. (2005) *Life Swap*. London: Michael Joseph Ltd.

Guldberg, Helene. (2009) *Reclaiming Childhood: Freedom and play in an age of fear*. London and New York: Routledge.

Hardyment, Christina. (2007) *Dream Babies: Childcare advice from John Locke to Gina Ford*. London: Francis Lincoln Publishers.

Hays, Sharon. (1996) *The Cultural Contradictions of Motherhood*. New Haven and London: Yale University Press.

Hewlett, Sylvia Ann. (2003) *Baby Hunger: The New Battle for Motherhood*. Atlantic Books.

Hochschild, Arlie Russell with Machung, Anne. (1989) *The Second Shift: Working parents and the revolution at home*. New York: Viking.

Kukla, Rebecca. (2005) *Mass Hysteria: Medicine, culture and mothers' bodies*. New York: Rowman and Littlefield Publishers.

Lasch, Christopher. (1977) *Haven in a Heartless World: The family besieged*. New York and London: Basic Books.

Layard, Richard and Dunn, Judy. (2009) *A Good Childhood: Searching for values in a competitive age*. London: Penguin.

Leach, Penelope. (1977) *Your Baby and Child*. London: Michael Joseph.

Lee, Ellie. (2003) *Abortion, Motherhood and Mental Health: Medicalising reproduction in the United States and Great Britain*. New York: Aldine de Gruyter.

Luik, John; Basham, Patrick; and Gori, Gio. (2006) *Diet Nation: Exposing the Obesity Crusade*. London: Social Affairs Unit.

Neill, Fiona. (2007) *The Secret Life of a Slummy Mummy*. London and New York: Century.

O'Farrell, John. (2005) *May Contain Nuts*. London: Doubleday.

Pearson, Allison. (2003) *I Don't Know How She Does It*. London: Vintage.

Piper, Heather and Stronach, Ian. (2008) *Don't Touch! The educational story of a panic*. London and New York: Routledge.

Schneider, Justine; Avis, Mark; and Leighton, Paul (Eds). (2007) *Supporting Children and Families: Lessons from Sure Start for Evidence-Based Practice in Health, Social Care and Education*. London and Philadelphia: Jessica Kingsley Publishers.

Shawne, Jennifer L. (2005) *Baby Not on Board: A Celebration of Life without Kids*. Chronicle Books.

Shriver, Lionel. (2005) *We Need To Talk About Kevin*. London: Serpent's Tail.

Spock, Benjamin and Parker, Stephen J. (1999) *Baby and Child Care*. London: Simon & Schuster.

Walker, Wendy. (2008) *Four Wives*. London: Arrow Books.

Warner, Judith. (2006) *Perfect Madness: Motherhood in an Age of Anxiety*. London: Vermilion.

Yates, Richard. (1961) *Revolutionary Road*. Little, Brown. [New edition: London: Vintage 2007].

Reports, Press Releases and Policy Documents

Bichard, Sir Michael. (2004: 22 June) The Bichard Inquiry Report. London: The Stationery Office http://police.homeoffice.gov.uk/publications/operational-policing/bichard-inquiry-report?view=Binary.

Blair, Tony. (2005: 2 December) 'Speech on improving parenting'. Number 10 website. Accessed 1 December 2007. http://www.pm.gov.uk/output/Page8123.asp.

The Children's Society. (2009a: Accessed 2 February) The Good Childhood Inquiry http://www.childrenssociety.org.uk/all_about_us/how_we_do_it/the_good_childhood_inquiry/1818.html.

The Children's Society. (2009b: 2 February) 'Excessive individualism threatens our children, say experts'. http://www.childrenssociety.org.uk/whats_happening/media_office/latest_news/14758_pr.html.

Daycare Trust. (2009) Childcare Costs Survey 2009. London: Daycare Trust http://www.daycaretrust.org.uk/mod/fileman/files/Costs_survey_2009.pdf.

DCSF (Department for Children, Schools and Families). (2008: 13 November) Children's Minister: Call on services to better support dads. http://www.dcsf.gov.uk/pns/DisplayPN.cgi?pn_id=2008_0254.

DCSF (Department for Children, Schools and Families). (2009: Accessed 31 January) 'Publications'. http://publications.dcsf.gov.uk/.

DCSF (Department for Children, Schools and Families). (2009: Accessed 7 February) 'Education-Related Parenting Contracts'. http://www.dcsf.gov.uk/schoolattendance/otherinitiatives/parentingcontracts.cfm.

DfES (Department for Education and Skills) (2007) Early Years Foundation Stage: Child Development Overview http://publications.teachernet.gov.uk/eOrderingDownload/DFES-00012-2007%20Cards.pdf.

DH (Department of Health) (2007) Birth to Five. London: Department of Health. http://www.dh.gov.uk/en/Publicationsandstatistics/Publications/PublicationsPolicyAndGuidance/dh_074924.

DH (Department of Health). (2008) 'Change 4 Life asks: "how are the kids?"' [Leaflet].

DIUS (Department of Innovation, Universities and Skills). (2007: October) Foresight: Tackling Obesities: Future Choices — Summary of Key Messages. London: Government Office for Science. http://kim.foresight.gov.uk/Obesity/obesity_final/20.pdf.

ECM (Every Child Matters). (2009a: Accessed 10 February). 'Aims and outcomes'. http://www.everychildmatters.gov.uk/aims/.

ECM (Every Child Matters). (2009b: Accessed 3 December) 'Background to Every Child Matters'. http://www.everychildmatters.gov.uk/aims/background/.

EYFS (Early Years Foundation Stage) (2009a: Accessed 10 February) 'EYFS Profile'. http://www.standards.dfes.gov.uk/eyfs/site/profile/index.htm.

EYFS (Early Years Foundation Stage) (2009b: Accessed 10 February) Early Years Foundation Stage Profile Assessment Scales Reference Sheet Poster. http://www.standards.dfes.gov.uk/eyfs/resources/downloads/assessment_scales_sheet.pdf.

Home Office. (1998) Supporting Families: A Consultation Document. London: The Stationery Office.

ISA (Independent Safeguarding Authority). (2009: Accessed 26 January) 'Your legal responsibilities'. http://www.isa-gov.org.uk/default.aspx?page=314.

ISA (Independent Safeguarding Authority). (2007: October) 'ISA Factsheet: Regulated and controlled activities'. http://www.isa-gov.org.uk/PDF/283896_ISA_A4_FactSheetNo3.pdf.

Laming, Lord. (2003: January) The Victoria Climbié Inquiry: Report. London: HMSO. http://www.victoria-climbie-inquiry.org.uk/finreport/finreport.htm.

NAPP (National Academy for Parenting Practitioners). (2007: 21 November) Press release: 'Launch of National Academy for Parenting Practitioners today signals a step change in driving up the quality of parent services'. http://www.parentingacademy.org/press.aspx?prid=8443cf74-db68-437b-9ff3-00ba7b7f3ce8.

Newiss, Geoff and Fairbrother, Lauren. (2004) 'Child abduction: understanding police recorded crime statistics'. Home Office. http://www.homeoffice.gov.uk/rds/pdfs2/r225.pdf.

ONS (2004) 'Life Expectancy: More aged 70 and 80 than ever before'. London: Office for National Statistics. http://www.statistics.gov.uk/cci/nugget.asp?id=881.

School Food Trust (2007: 3 September) 'Press Release: Packed lunches falling behind school dinners as nutritional gap widens'. http://www.schoolfoodtrust.org.uk/news_item.asp?NewsId=92.

UNICEF (2007) Report Card 7: Child poverty in perspective: An overview of child well-being in rich countries. Florence: Innocenti Research Centre http://www.unicef-irc.org/publications/pdf/rc7_eng.pdf.

UNICEF (2008) Report Card 8: The Child Care Transition: A league table of early childhood education and care in economically advanced countries. Florence: Innocenti Research Centre http://www.unicef-irc.org/publications/pdf/rc8_eng.pdf.

Articles

Allen-Mills, Tony. (2006: 12 November) 'Martini Moms toast a rebellion against parental correctness' *The Sunday Times*.

BBC News Online (2001: 19 November) 'Climbie officer "feared scabies"'.

BBC News Online (2007: 26 March) 'Cameron orders childhood inquiry'.

BBC News Online (2007: 5 May) 'Head teachers demand test reforms'.

BBC News Online. (2007: 25 May) '"No alcohol in pregnancy" advised'.

BBC News Online (2007: 4 September) 'Tougher rules for excluded pupils'.

Belsky, J; Melhuish, Edward; Barnes, Jacqueline; Leyland, Alastair H; Romaniuk, Helena. (2006) 'Effects of Sure Start local programmes on children and families: early findings from a quasi-experimental, cross sectional study' *British Medical Journal* 2006; 332:1476.

Bennett, Rosemary. (2007: 4 October) 'Maternity expert Claire Verity is asked to stay away from Baby Show as mothers threaten protest' *The Times* (London).

Bennett, Rosemary and Frean, Alexandra. (2009: 27 January) 'Alarm over security of children's database' *The Times* (London).

Bristow, Jennie. (2005: 14 June) 'We don't need to talk about hating our kids'. *spiked*.

Bristow, Jennie. (2007: 27 May) 'Guide to Subversive Parenting. Rule 3: Pregnancy does not damage your child'. *spiked*.

Britten, Fleur. (2008: 29 June) 'Katie Roiphe: Why you shouldn't let your kids rule your life' *Sunday Times* (London).

Byron, Tanya. (2007: 30 August) 'Bringing up children — your way' *The Times* (London).

Casciani, Dominic. (2008: 31 January) 'Analysis: UK gun crime figures'. BBC News Online.

Casciani, Dominic. (2008: 15 September) 'Sex offender alerts plan launched'. BBC News Online.

Clark, Ross. (2004: 24 June) 'The lessons of Soham inspired by the spirit of Salem'. *The Times* (London).

Daily Mail (2007: 29 October) 'TV "baby guru" Claire Verity to be quizzed over qualifications'.

Daily Mail. (2008: 1 October) 'Parents "are so concerned with being perfect that a generation of kids is growing up spoilt"'.

Daily Mirror (2006: 22 March) 'Mum's agony as she finds tot, 2, under water'.

Daily Telegraph (2007: 3 August) 'Mothers warned holiday stress could drive them to drink'.

Driscoll, Margarette. (2008: 7 September) 'Why these women and top jobs aren't mixing'. *The Sunday Times*.

Epstein, Joseph. (2008: 9 June) 'The Kindergarchy: Every child a dauphin'. *The Weekly Standard*, Volume 013, Issue 37.

Finkelstein, Daniel. (2009: 4 February) 'Happily, children don't have such a hard time'. *The Times* (London).

Fitzpatrick, Dr Michael. (2008: 8 October) 'Childhood obesity is not a form of child abuse' *spiked*.

Frean, Alexandra. (2008: 11 December) Childcare is bad for your baby, working parents are warned. *The Times* (London).

Fulford, Kishanda. (2007: 3 August) 'Of course mothers are driven to drink'. *Daily Telegraph* (London).

Furedi, Frank. (2008: 5 September) 'Moralisers on a PC witch-hunt.' *The Australian*.

Garavelli, Dani. (2007: 7 October) 'What side are you on in the baby wars?' *Scotland on Sunday*.

Gilbert, Ruth; Spatz Widom, Cathy; Browne, Kevin; Fergusson, David; Webb, Elspeth; Janson, Staffan, Janson. (2009: 3 January) 'Burden and consequences of child maltreatment in high-income countries.' *The Lancet*, Volume 373, Issue 9657, Pages 68 – 81.

Goodwin, Daisy. (2009: 1 February) 'Our children's blighted lives.' *The Sunday Times* (London).

Guardian (2004: 22 June) 'Bichard report: reaction in quotes'.

Hartley-Brewer, Julia. (2007: 26 August) 'Time for parents to tame their tearaways'. *Sunday Express* (London).

Hill, Amelia. (2007: 7 October) 'Baby guru steps up pressure on TV rival: Gina Ford complains to the NSPCC over the "child abuse" seen on Claire Verity's C4 show'. *The Observer* (London).

Hill, Amelia; Davies, Caroline; and Hinsliff, Gaby. (2009: 1 February) 'Are our children really in crisis, or the victims of parents' anxiety?' *The Observer* (London).

Hope, Christopher. (2007: 25 September) 'Jack Straw admits: We made a mistake on cannabis.' *The Daily Telegraph* (London).

Hope, Jenny. (2008: 4 December) 'Are one in 10 children REALLY being abused? Huge doubts over major new study.' *Daily Mail* (London).

Independent. (2004: 9 September) 'Cherie Blair immortalised in quote collection'.

Johnson, Rachel. (2009: 18 January) 'Parents' playpen coup'. *The Sunday Times* (London).
http://www.timesonline.co.uk/tol/comment/columnists/rachel_johnson/article5537303.ece.

Kavanagh, Marianne. (2008: 26 November) 'Mothers need me-time, too.' *Daily Telegraph* (London).
http://www.telegraph.co.uk/family/3527073/Mothers-need-me-time-to.html.

Kukla, Rebecca. (2007: May) 'Measuring Mothering: philosophical and sociological perspectives on intensive mothering.' Paper given at the conference Monitoring Parents: childrearing in an age of 'intensive parenting', University of Kent, May 2007.

Leach, Penelope. (2008: 14 December) 'This is the mother of all childcare fallacies'. *Sunday Times* (London).

Littlemore, Sue. (2007: 20 November) 'Learning how to be a good parent.' BBC News Online.

Lyons, Rob. (2006: 18 September) 'Jamie Oliver: what a "tosser"'. *spiked*.

McCartney, Jenny. (2007: 29 April) 'Ass-straightening for beginners'. *Sunday Telegraph* (London).

McDermott, Nancy. (2007: 3 August) 'Parents take parenting far too seriously'. *spiked*.

Munro, Eileen. (2003: 10 September) 'This would not have saved Victoria.' *Guardian* (London).

Obama, Michelle. (2008: 7 November) 'My No 1 job as First Lady is to be First Mom'. *The Times* (London).

Obama, Barack. (2009: 15 January) 'Barack Obama: a letter to my girls'. *Sunday Times* (London).

Segrave, Elisa. (1997: 3 December) 'Parents: You'll do it their way.' *Guardian* (London).

Sylvester, Rachel and Thomson, Alice. (2007: 2 June) 'State supernanny lays down the law: The "respect tsar" tells Rachel Sylvester and Alice

Thomson that one of her aims is to bring discipline back to British life. *Daily Telegraph* (London).

Templeton, Sarah-Kate. (2007: 7 May) 'Children "bad for planet"'. *The Australian*.

Templeton, Sarah-Kate. (2009: 1 February) 'Two children should be limit, says green guru'. *The Sunday Times* (London).

Thomas, Lesley. (2009: 24 January) 'Rachida Dati might simply have been trying to save her job'. *The Times* (London).

Toynbee, Polly. (2005: 13 September) 'We must hold our nerve and support deprived children'. *Guardian* (London).

Tucker, Emma. (2007: 20 August) 'Enfants terribles: Interview with Corinne Maier'. *The Times* (London).

Turner, Janice. (2009: 10 January) 'Women, resist the siren call of the cupcake!' *The Times* (London).

UPI News Service. (2006: 26 August) 'British "Supernanny" family blame depiction for community backlash'.

Waiton, Stuart. (2006: 19 January) Antisocial behaviour: the construction of a crime. *spiked*.

Ward, Lucy. (2005: 13 September) 'Doubts over value of £3bn Sure Start'. *Guardian* (London).

Woolcock, Nicola. (2008: 24 July) 'Authors unite against drive for toddler literacy'. *The Times* (London).

Websites

Alcohol Policy UK. (2007: 16 June). 'New alcohol guidelines for pregnant women: where's the evidence?' Accessed 12 February 2009. http://www.alcoholpolicy.net/2007/06/new_alcohol_gui.html.

Bad Mothers Club. (2009: Accessed 7 February) 'Why BMC?' http://www.badmothersclub.co.uk/jsp/index.jsp?lnk=001.

Bad Mothers Club. (2009b: Accessed 7 February) 'Bollocks of the Week: PND! La Leche! Bollocks!' http://www.badmothersclub.co.uk/jsp/index.jsp?lnk=110&category=Bollocks%20of%20the%20Week.

Childfree.net. (2009: Accessed 23 January) http://www.childfree.net/.

Jo Frost. (2009: Accessed 23 February) 'ABOUT B4UGo-Ga-Ga'. http://www.jofrost.com/jo_frost_b4ugo-ga-ga.php#services.

Netmums. (2007: Accessed 7 February) A Mum's Life. http://www.netmums.com/campaigns/A_Mum_s_Life.656/.

NSPCC. (2009: Accessed 25 January) 'Child abductions: Key child protection statistics (December 2007)'. http://www.nspcc.org.uk/Inform/resourcesforprofessionals/Statistics/KeyCPStats/15_wda48733.html.

Parentline Plus. (2009: Accessed 7 February) http://www.parentlineplus.org.uk.

School Food Trust. (2009: Accessed 7 February) 'About the Trust'. http://www.schoolfoodtrust.org.uk/content.asp?ContentId=232.

2008–2009

SOCIETAS

essays in political and cultural criticism

imprint-academic.com/societas

Who Holds the Moral High Ground?

Colin J Beckley and Elspeth Waters

Meta-ethical attempts to define concepts such as 'goodness', 'right and wrong', 'ought' and 'ought not', have proved largely futile, even over-ambitious. Morality, it is argued, should therefore be directed primarily at the reduction of suffering, principally because the latter is more easily recognisable and accords with an objective view and requirements of the human condition. All traditional and contemporary perspectives are without suitable criteria for evaluating moral dilemmas and without such guidance we face the potent threat of sliding to a destructive moral nihilism. This book presents a possible set of defining characteristics for the foundation of moral evaluations, taking into consideration that the female gender may be better disposed to ethical leadership.

128 pp., £8.95/$17.90, 9781845401030 (pbk.), January 2008, *Societas,* Vol.32

Froude Today

John Coleman

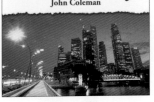

A.L. Rowse called fellow-historian James Anthony Froude the 'last great Victorian awaiting revival'. The question of power is the problem that perplexes every age: in his historical works Froude examined how it applied to the Tudor period, and defended Carlyle against the charge that he held the doctrine that 'Might is Right'.

Froude applied his analysis of power to the political classes of his own time and that is why his writings are just as relevant today. The historian and the prophet look into the inner meaning of events – and that is precisely what Froude did – and so are able to make judgments which apply to ages far beyond their own. The last chapters imagine what Froude would have said had he been here today.

96 pp., £8.95/$17.90, 9781845401047 (pbk.), March 2008, *Societas,* Vol.33

Imprint Academic, PO Box 200, Exeter EX5 5HY, UK
Tel: +44(0)1392 851550.   Email: sandra@imprint.co.uk

The Enemies of Progress

Austin Williams

This polemical book examines the concept of sustainability and presents a critical exploration of its all-pervasive influence on society, arguing that sustainability, manifested in several guises, represents a pernicious and corrosive doctrine that has survived primarily because there seems to be no alternative to its canon: in effect, its bi-partisan appeal has depressed critical engagement and neutered politics.

It is a malign philosophy of misanthropy, low aspirations and restraint. This book argues for a destruction of the mantra of sustainability, removing its unthinking status as orthodoxy, and for the reinstatement of the notions of development, progress, experimentation and ambition in its place.

Al Gore insists that the 'debate is over'. Here the auhtor retorts that it is imperative to argue against the moralizing of politics.

Austin Williams tutors at the Royal College of Art and Bartlett School of Architecture.

96 pp., £8.95/$17.90, 9781845400989 (pbk.), May 2008, *Societas*, Vol.34

Forgiveness: How Religion Endangers Morality

R.A. Sharpe

In his book *The Moral Case against Religious Belief* (1997), the author argued that some important virtues cease to be virtues at all when set in a religious context, and that, consequently, a religious life is, in many respects, not a good life to lead. In this sequel, his tone is less generous to believers than hitherto, because 'the intervening decade has brought home to us the terrible results of religious conviction'.

R.A. Sharpe was Professor Emeritus at St David's College, Lampeter. The manuscript of *Forgiveness* was prepared for publication by his widow, the philosopher Lynne Sharpe.

128 pp., £8.95 / $17.90, 9781845400835 (pbk.), July 2008, (*Societas* edition), Vol.35

To qualify for the reduced (subscription) price of £5/$10 for current and future volumes (£2.50/$5.00 for back volumes), please use the enclosed direct debit form or order via imprint-academic.com/societas

Healing, Hype or Harm? Scientists Investigate Complementary or Alternative Medicine

Edzard Ernst (ed.)

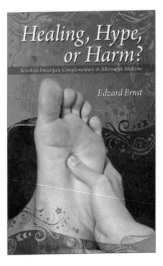

The scientists writing this book are not 'against' complementary or alternative medicine (CAM), but they are very much 'for' evidence-based medicine and single standards. They aim to counter-balance the many uncritical books on CAM and to stimulate intelligent, well-informed public debate.

TOPICS INCLUDE: What is CAM? Why is it so popular? Patient choice; Reclaiming compassion; Teaching CAM at university; Research on CAM; CAM in court; Ethics and CAM; Politics and CAM; Homeopathy in context; Concepts of holism in medicine; Placebo, deceit and CAM; Healing but not curing; CAM and the media.

Edzard Ernst is Professor of Complementary Medicine, Universities of Exeter and Plymouth.

190 pp., £8.95/$17.90, 9781845401184 (pbk.), Sept. 2008, *Societas,* Vol.36

The Balancing Act: National Identity and Sovereignty for Britain in Europe

Atsuko Ichijo

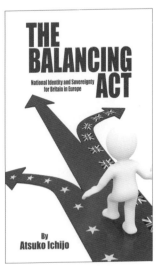

This is a careful examination of the historical formation of Britain and of key moments in its relations with the European powers. The author looks at the governing discourses of politicians, the mass media, and the British people.

The rhetoric of sovereignty among political elites and the population at large is found to conceive of Britain's engagement with Europe as a zero-sum game. A second theme is the power of geographical images – island Britain – in feeding the idea of the British nation as by nature separate and autonomous. It follows that the EU is seen as 'other' and involvement in European decision-making tends to be viewed in terms of threat. This is naive, as nation-states are not autonomous, economically, militarily or politically. Only pooling sovereignty can maximize their national interests.

Atsuko Ichijo is Senior Researcher in European Studies at Kingston University.

150 pp., £8.95/$17.90, 9781845401153 (pbk.), Nov. 2008, *Societas,* Vol.37

Seeking Meaning and Making Sense

John Haldane

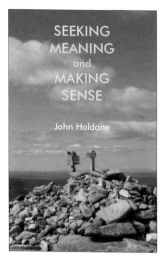

Here is an engaging collection of short essays that range across philosophy, politics, general culture, morality, science, religion and art.

The author contributes regularly to *The Scotsman* and a number of radio programmes. Many of these essays began life in this way, and retain their direct fresh style.

The focus is on questions of Meaning, Value and Understanding. Topics include: Making sense of religion, Making sense of society, Making sense of evil, Making sense of art and science, Making sense of nature.

John Haldane is Professor of Philosophy and Director of the Centre for Ethics, Philosophy and Public Affairs in the University of St Andrews.

128 pp., £8.95/$17.90, 9781845401221 (pbk.), Jan. 2009, *Societas,* Vol.38

Independent: The Rise of the Non-aligned Politician

Richard Berry

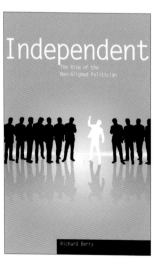

Martin Bell, Ken Livingstone and Richard Taylor (the doctor who became an MP to save his local hospital) are the best known of a growing band of British politicians making their mark outside the traditional party system.

Some (like Livingstone) have emerged from within the old political system that let them down, others (Bell, Taylor) have come into politics from outside in response to a crisis of some kind, often in defence of a perceived threat to their local town or district.

Richard Berry traces this development by case studies and interviews to test the theory that these are not isolated cases, but part of a permanent trend in British politics, a shift away from the party system in favour of independent non-aligned representatives of the people.

Richard Berry is a political and policy researcher and writer.

128 pp., £8.95/$17.90, 9781845401283 (pbk.), March 2009, *Societas,* Vol.39

Progressive Secular Society and other essays relevant to secularism

Tom Rubens

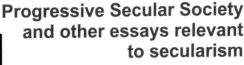
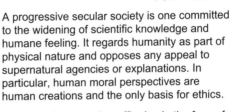

A progressive secular society is one committed to the widening of scientific knowledge and humane feeling. It regards humanity as part of physical nature and opposes any appeal to supernatural agencies or explanations. In particular, human moral perspectives are human creations and the only basis for ethics.

Secular values need re-affirming in the face of the resurgence of aggressive supernatural religious doctrines and practices. This book gives a set of 'secular thoughts for the day' – many only a page or two long – on topics as varied as Shakespeare and Comte, economics, science and social action.

Tom Rubens teaches in the humanities at secondary and tertiary levels.

128 pp., £8.95/$17.90, 9781845401320 (pbk.), May 2009, *Societas,* Vol.40

Self and Society (enlarged second edition)

William Irwin Thompson

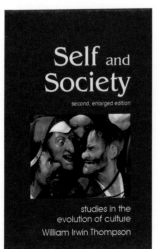

The book contains a series of essays on the evolution of culture, dealing with topics including the city and consciousness, evolution of the afterlife, literary and mathematical archetypes, machine consciousness and the implications of 9/11 and the invasion of Iraq for the development of planetary culture.

This enlarged edition contains an additional new second part, added to include chapters on 'Natural Drift and the Evolution of Culture' and 'The Transition from Nation-State to Noetic Polity' as well as two shorter reflective pieces.

The author is a poet, cultural historian and founder of the Lindisfarne Association. His many books include *Coming into Being: Artifacts and Texts in the Evolution of Consciousness.*

150 pp., £8.95/$17.90, 9781845401337 (pbk.), July 2009, *Societas,* Vol.41

Universities: The Recovery of an Idea (revised second edition)

Gordon Graham

RAE, teaching quality assessment, student course evaluation, modularization – these are all names of innovations in modern British universities. How far do they constitute a significant departure from traditional academic concerns? Using themes from J.H.Newman's *The Idea of a University* as a starting point, this book aims to address these questions.

'It is extraordinary how much Graham has managed to say (and so well) in a short book.' **Alasdair MacIntyre**

£8.95/$17.90, 9781845401276 (pbk), *Societas* V.1

God in Us: A Case for Christian Humanism

Anthony Freeman

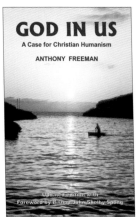

God In Us is a radical representation of the Christian faith for the 21st century. Following the example of the Old Testament prophets and the first-century Christians it overturns received ideas about God. God is not an invisible person 'out there' somewhere, but lives in the human heart and mind as 'the sum of all our values and ideals' guiding and inspiring our lives.

The Revd. Anthony Freeman was dismissed from his parish for publishing this book, but remains a priest in the Church of England.

'Brilliantly lucid.' *Philosophy Now*
'A brave and very well-written book' *The Freethinker*

£8.95/$17.90, 9780907845171 (pbk), *Societas* V.2

The Case Against the Democratic State

Gordon Graham

This essay contends that the gross imbalance of power in the modern state is in need of justification and that democracy simply masks this need with the illusion of popular sovereignty. The book points out the emptiness of slogans like 'power to the people', as individual votes do not affect the outcome of elections, but concludes that democracy can contribute to civic education.

'Challenges the reigning orthodoxy'. *Mises Review*

'Political philosophy in the best analytic tradition… scholarly, clear, and it does not require a professional philosopher to understand it' *Philosophy Now*

'An excellent candidate for inclusion on an undergraduate syllabus.' *Independent Review*

£8.95/$17.90, 9780907845386 (pbk), *Societas* V.3

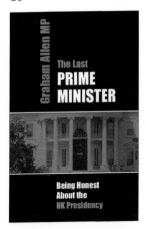

The Last Prime Minister
Graham Allen MP

This book shows how Britain has acquired an executive presidency by stealth. It is the first ever attempt to codify the Prime Minister's powers, many hidden in the mysteries of the royal prerogative. This timely second edition takes in new issues, including Parliament's impotence over Iraq.

'Iconoclastic, stimulating and well-argued.' **Vernon Bogdanor**, *Times Higher Education Supplement*

'Well-informed and truly alarming.' **Peter Hennessy**

'Should be read by anybody interested in the constitution.' **Anthony King**

£8.95/$17.90, 9780907845416 (pbk), *Societas* V.4

The Liberty Option
Tibor R. Machan

The Liberty Option advances the idea that it is the society organised on classical liberal principles that serves justice best, leads to prosperity and encourages the greatest measure of individual virtue. The book contrasts this Lockean ideal with the various statist alternatives, defends it against its communitarian critics and lays out some of its more significant policy implications. The author teaches ethics at Chapman University. His books on classical liberal theory include *Classical Individualism* (Routledge, 1998).

£8.95/$17.90, 9780907845638 (pbk), *Societas* V.5

Democracy, Fascism & the New World Order
Ivo Mosley

Growing up as the grandson of Sir Oswald, the 1930s blackshirt leader, made Ivo Mosley consider fascism with a deep and acutely personal interest. Whereas conventional wisdom sets up democracy and fascism as opposites, to ancient political theorists democracy had an innate tendency to lead to extreme populist government, and provided unscrupulous demagogues with the ideal opportunity to seize power. In *Democracy, Fascism and the New World Order* Mosley argues that totalitarian regimes may well be the logical outcome of unfettered mass democracy.

'Brings a passionate reasoning to the analysis'. *Daily Mail*

'Read Mosley's, in many ways, excellent book. But read it critically.' **Edward Ingram**, *Philosophy Now*

£8.95/$17.90, 9780907845645 (pbk), *Societas* V.6

Off With Their Wigs!
Charles Banner and Alexander Deane

On June 12, 2003, a press release concerning a Cabinet reshuffle declared as a footnote that the ancient office of Lord Chancellor was to be abolished and that a new supreme court would replace the House of Lords as the highest appeal court. This book critically analyses the Government's proposals and looks at the various alternative models for appointing judges and for a new court of final appeal.

'A cogently argued critique.' *Commonwealth Lawyer*

£8.95/$17.90, 9780907845843 (pbk), *Societas* V.7

The Modernisation Imperative
Bruce Charlton & Peter Andras

Modernisation gets a bad press in the UK, and is blamed for increasing materialism, moral fragmentation, the dumbing-down of public life, declining educational standards, occupational insecurity and rampant managerialism. But modernisation is preferable to the likely alternative of lapsing back towards a 'medieval' world of static, hierarchical and coercive societies – the many and serious criticisms of modernisation should be seen as specific problems relating to a process that is broadly beneficial for most of the people, most of the time.

'A powerful and new analysis'. **Matt Ridley**

£8.95/$17.90, 9780907845522 (pbk), *Societas* V.8

Self and Society, *William Irwin Thompson*

£8.95/$17.90, 9780907845829 (pbk), *Societas* V.9
now superceded by Vol.41 (see above, p.S6)

The Party's Over
Keith Sutherland

This book questions the role of the party in the post-ideological age and concludes that government ministers should be appointed by headhunters and held to account by a parliament selected by lot.

'Sutherland's model of citizen's juries ought to have much greater appeal to progressive Britain.' *Observer*

'An extremely valuable contribution.' *Tribune*

'A political essay in the best tradition – shrewd, erudite, polemical, partisan, mischievous and highly topical.' *Contemporary Political Theory*

£8.95/$17.90, 9780907845515 (pbk), *Societas* V.10

Our Last Great Illusion

Rob Weatherill

This book aims to refute, primarily through the prism of modern psychoanalysis and postmodern theory, the notion of a return to nature, to holism, or to a pre-Cartesian ideal of harmony and integration. Far from helping people, therapy culture's utopian solutions may be a cynical distraction, creating delusions of hope. Yet solutions proliferate in the free market; this is why therapy is our last great illusion. The author is a psychoanalytic psychotherapist and lecturer, Trinity College, Dublin.

'Challenging, but well worth the engagement.' *Network*

£8.95/$17.90, 9780907845959 (pbk), *Societas* V.11

The Snake that Swallowed its Tail

Mark Garnett

Liberal values are the hallmark of a civilised society, but depend on an optimistic view of the human condition, Stripped of this essential ingredient, liberalism has become a hollow abstraction. Tracing its effects through the media, politics and the public services, the book argues that hollowed-out liberalism has helped to produce our present discontent.

'This arresting account will be read with profit by anyone interested in the role of ideas in politics.' **John Gray**, *New Statesman*

'A spirited polemic addressing the malaise of British politics.' **Michael Freeden**, *The European Legacy*

£8.95/$17.90, 9780907845881 (pbk), *Societas* V.12

Why the Mind is Not a Computer

Raymond Tallis

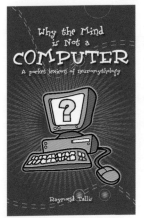

The equation 'Mind = Machine' is false. This pocket lexicon of 'neuromythology' shows why. Taking a series of keywords such as calculation, language, information and memory, Professor Tallis shows how their misuse has a misled a generation. First of all these words were used literally in the description of the human mind. Then computer scientists applied them metaphorically to the workings of machines. And finally the use of the terms was called as evidence of artificial intelligence in machines *and* the computational nature of thought.

'A splendid exception to the helpless specialisation of our age' **Mary Midgley**, *THES*

'A work of radical clarity.' *J. Consciousness Studies*

£8.95/$17.90, 9780907845942 (pbk), *Societas* V.13

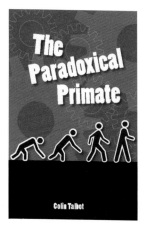

The Paradoxical Primate
Colin Talbot

This book seeks to explain how human beings can be so malleable, yet have an inherited set of instincts. When E.O. Wilson's *Consilience* made a plea for greater integration, it was assumed that the traffic would be from physical to human science. Talbot reverses this assumption and reviews some of the most innovative developments in evolutionary psychology, ethology and behavioural genetics.

'Talbot's ambition is admirable...a framework that can simultaneously encompass individualism and concern for collective wellbeing.' *Public* (The Guardian)

£8.95/$17.90, 9780907845850 (pbk), *Societas* V.14

Tony Blair and the Ideal Type
J.H. Grainger

The 'ideal type' is Max Weber's hypothetical leading democratic politician, whom the author finds realized in Tony Blair. He is a politician emerging from no obvious mould, treading no well-beaten path to high office, and having few affinities of tone, character or style with his predecessors. He is the Outsider or Intruder, not belonging to the 'given' of British politics and dedicated to its transformation. (The principles outlined are also applicable. across the parties, in the post-Blair period.) The author was reader in political science at the Australian National University and is the author of *Character and Style in English Politics* (CUP).

'A brilliant essay.' **Simon Jenkins**, *Sunday Times*
'A scintillating case of the higher rudeness.' *Guardian*

£8.95/$17.90, 9781845400248 (pbk), *Societas* V.15

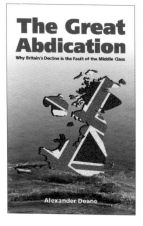

The Great Abdication
Alex Deane

According to Deane, Britain's middle class has abstained from its responsibility to uphold societal values, resulting in the collapse of our society's norms and standards. The middle classes must reinstate themselves as arbiters of morality, be unafraid to judge their fellow men, and follow through with the condemnation that follows when individuals sin against common values.

'[Deane] thinks there is still an element in the population which has traditional middle-class values. Well, maybe.' **George Wedd**, *Contemporary Review*

£8.95/$17.90, 9780907845973 (pbk), *Societas* V.16

Neil MacCormick

Who's Afraid of a
European
Constitution?

Who's Afraid of a European Constitution?

Neil MacCormick

This book discusses how the EU Constitution was drafted, whether it promised any enhancement of democracy in the EU and whether it implied that the EU is becoming a superstate. The arguments are equally of interest regarding the EU Reform Treaty.

Sir Neil MacCormick is professor of public law at Edinburgh University. He was an MEP and a member of the Convention on the Future of Europe.

£8.95/$17.90, 9781845392 (pbk), *Societas* V.17

Darwinian Conservatism

Larry Arnhart

DARWINIAN
Conservatism

Larry Arnhart

The Left has traditionally assumed that human nature is so malleable, so perfectible, that it can be shaped in almost any direction. Conservatives object, arguing that social order arises not from rational planning but from the spontaneous order of instincts and habits. Darwinian biology sustains conservative social thought by showing how the human capacity for spontaneous order arises from social instincts and a moral sense shaped by natural selection. The author is professor of political science at Northern Illinois University.

'Strongly recommended.' *Salisbury Review*

'An excellect book.' **Anthony Flew**, *Right Now!*

'Conservative critics of Darwin ignore Arnhart at their own peril.' *Review of Politics*

96 pp., £8.95/$17.90, 9780907845997 (pbk.), *Societas,* Vol. 18

Doing Less With Less: Making Britain More Secure

Paul Robinson

Doing Less with Less
Making Britain More Secure

Paul Robinson

Notwithstanding the rhetoric of the 'war on terror', the world is now a far safer place. However, armed forces designed for the Cold War encourage global interference through pre-emption and other forms of military interventionism. We would be safer with less. The author, an ex-army officer, is assistant director of the Centre for Security Studies at Hull University.

'Robinson's criticisms need to be answered.'
Tim Garden, *RUSI Journal*

'The arguments in this thesis should be acknowledged by the MOD.' **Major General Patrick Cordingley DSO**

£8.95/$17.90, 9781845400422 (pbk), *Societas* V.19

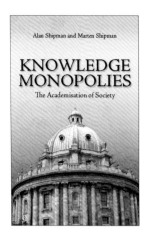

Knowledge Monopolies
Alan Shipman & Marten Shipman

Historians and sociologists chart the *consequences* of the expansion of knowledge; philosophers of science examine the *causes*. This book bridges the gap. The focus is on the paradox whereby, as the general public becomes better educated to live and work with knowledge, the 'academy' increases its intellectual distance, so that the nature of reality becomes more rather than less obscure.

'A deep and searching look at the successes and failures of higher education.' *Commonwealth Lawyer*

'A must read.' *Public* (The Guardian)

£8.95/$17.90, 9781845400286 (pbk), *Societas* V.20

The Referendum Roundabout
Kieron O'Hara

A lively and sharp critique of the role of the referendum in modern British politics. The 1975 vote on Europe is the lens to focus the subject, and the controversy over the referendum on the European constitution is also in the author's sights.

The author is a senior research fellow at the University of Southampton and author of *Plato and the Internet*, *Trust: From Socrates to Spin* and *After Blair: Conservatism Beyond Thatcher* (2005).

£8.95/$17.90, 9781845400408 (pbk), *Societas* V.21

The Moral Mind
Henry Haslam

The reality and validity of the moral sense took a battering in the last century. Materialist trends in philosophy, the decline in religious faith, and a loosening of traditional moral constraints added up to a shift in public attitudes, leaving many people aware of a questioning of moral claims and uneasy with a world that has no place for the morality. Haslam shows how important the moral sense is to the human personality and exposes the weakness in much current thinking that suggests otherwise.

'Marking a true advance in the discussion of evolutionary explanations of morality, this book is highly recommended for all collections.' **David Gordon**, *Library Journal*

'An extremely sensible little book. It says things that are really rather obvious, but which have somehow got forgotten.' **Mary Midgley**

£8.95/$17.90, 9781845400163 (pbk), *Societas* V.22

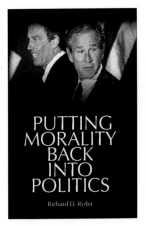

Putting Morality Back Into Politics *Richard D. Ryder*

Ryder argues that the time has come for public policies to be seen to be based upon moral objectives. Politicians should be expected routinely to justify their policies with open moral argument. In Part I, Ryder sketches an overview of contemporary political philosophy as it relates to the moral basis for politics, and Part 2 suggests a way of putting morality back into politics, along with a clearer emphasis upon scientific evidence. Trained as a psychologist, the author has also been a political lobbyist, mostly in relation to animal welfare.

£8.95/$17.90, 9781845400477 (pbk), *Societas* V.23

Village Democracy
John Papworth

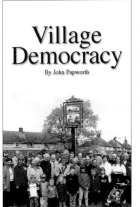

'A civilisation that genuinely reflects all that human beings long for and aspire to can only be created on the basis of each person's freely acknowledged power to decide on each of the many questions that affect his life.' In the forty years since he wrote those words in the first issue of his journal *Resurgence*, John Papworth has not wavered from that belief. This latest book passionately restates his argument for radical decentralisation.

'If we are to stand any chance of surviving we need to heed Papworth's call for decentralisation.'
Zac Goldsmith, *The Ecologist*

£8.95/$17.90, 9781845400644 (pbk), *Societas* V.24

Debating Humanism
Dolan Cummings (ed.)

Broadly speaking, the humanist tradition is one in which it is we as human beings who decide for ourselves what is best for us, and are responsible for shaping our own societies. For humanists, then, debate is all the more important, not least at a time when there is discussion about the unexpected return of religion as a political force. This collection of essays follows the Institute of Ideas' inaugural 2005 Battle of Ideas festival. Contributors include Josie Appleton, Simon Blackburn, Robert Brecher, Andrew Copson, Dylan Evans, Revd. Anthony Freeman, Frank Furedi, A.C. Grayling, Dennis Hayes, Elisabeth Lasch-Quinn, Kenan Malik and Daphne Patai.

£8.95/$17.90, 9781845400699 (pbk), *Societas* V.25

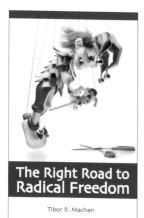

The Right Road to Radical Freedom *Tibor R. Machan*

This work focuses on the topic of free will – do we as individual human beings choose our conduct, at least partly independently, freely? He comes down on the side of libertarians who answer Yes, and scorns the compatibilism of philosophers like Daniel Dennett, who try to rescue some kind of freedom from a physically determined universe. From here he moves on to apply his belief in radical freedom to areas of life such as religion, politics, and morality, tackling subjects as diverse as taxation, private property, justice and the welfare state.

£8.95/$17.90, 9781845400187 (pbk), *Societas* V.26

Paradoxes of Power: Reflections on the Thatcher Interlude
Sir Alfred Sherman

In her memoirs Lady Thatcher herself pays tribute to her former adviser's 'brilliance', the 'force and clarity of his mind', his 'breadth of reading and his skills as a ruthless polemicist'. She credits him with a central role in her achievements. Born in 1919 in London's East End, until 1948 Sherman was a Communist and fought in the Spanish Civil War. But he ended up a free-market crusader.

'These reflections by Thatcherism's inventor are necessary reading.' **John Hoskyns**, *Salisbury Review*

£8.95/$17.90, 9781845400927 (pbk), *Societas* V.27

Public Health & Globalisation
Iain Brassington

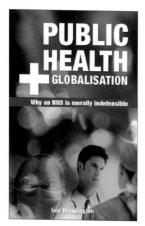

This book claims that the NHS is morally indefensible. There is a good moral case in favour of a *public* health service, but these arguments do not point towards a *national* health service, but to something that looks far more like a *transnational* health service. Drawing on Peter Singer's famous arguments in favour of a duty of rescue, the author argues that the cost of the NHS is unjustifiable. If we accept a duty to save lives when the required sacrifice is small, then we ought also to accept sacrifices in the NHS in favour of foreign aid. This does not imply that the NHS is wrong; just that it is wrong to spend large amounts on one person in Britain when we could save more lives elsewhere.

£8.95/$17.90, 9781845400798 (pbk), *Societas* V.28

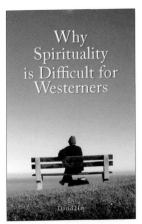

Why Spirituality is Difficult for Westerners *David Hay*

Zoologist David Hay holds that religious or spiritual awareness is biologically natural to the human species and has been selected for in organic evolution because it has survival value. Although naturalistic, this hypothesis is not intended to be reductionist. Indeed, it implies that all people have a spiritual life. This book describes the historical and economic context of European secularism, and considers recent developments in neurophysiology of the brain as it relates to religious experience.

£8.95/$17.90, 9781845400484 (pbk), *Societas* V.29

Earthy Realism: The Meaning of GAIA
Mary Midgley (ed.)

GAIA, named after the ancient Greek mother-goddess, is the notion that the Earth and the life on it form an active, self-maintaining whole. It has a *scientific* side, as shown by the new university departments of earth science which bring biology and geology together to study the continuity of the cycle. It also has a visionary or *spiritual* aspect. What the contributors to this book believe is needed is to bring these two angles together. With global warming now an accepted fact, the lessons of GAIA have never been more relevant and urgent. Foreword by James Lovelock.

£8.95/$17.90, 9781845400804 (pbk), *Societas* V.30

Joseph Conrad Today
Kieron O'Hara

This book argues that the novelist Joseph Conrad's work speaks directly to us in a way that none of his contemporaries can. Conrad's scepticism, pessimism, emphasis on the importance and fragility of community, and the difficulties of escaping our history are important tools for understanding the political world in which we live. He is prepared to face a future where progress is not inevitable, where actions have unintended consequences, and where we cannot know the contexts in which we act. The result can hardly be called a political programme, but Conrad's work is clearly suggestive of a sceptical conservatism of the sort described by the author in his 2005 book *After Blair: Conservatism Beyond Thatcher*.

£8.95/$17.90, 9781845400668 (pbk.), *Societas* V.31